D1454045

POLICE INTELLIGENCE

POLICE INTELLIGENCE

The Operations
of
an Investigative Unit

by

ANTHONY V. BOUZA

AMS Press, Inc.
New York
1976

PUBLICATION HISTORY

Library of Congress Cataloguing in Publication Data
Bouza, Anthony V
    Police Intelligence.
    Bibliography: p.179
    1. New York (City). Police Dept. Bureau of Special Services. 2. New York (City)—Police. 3. Intelligence service—New York (City)
    I. Title.
HV8148.N52B68   363.2'32   75-8667

ISBN 0-404-13138-7

Manufactured in the United States of America

DEDICATION

For my mother, Encarnacion Bouza.

Table of Contents

I.	Introductions	3
II.	Mandate and History	14
III.	Administration and Personnel	29
IV.	Subversion	50
V.	Security for Dignitaries	96
VI.	Labor Disputes	121
VII.	Liaisons and Policy	138
VIII.	Redirections	160
	Notes	171
	Bibliography	179
	Index	185

POLICE INTELLIGENCE

The Operations
of
an Investigative Unit

Introductions

For the Bureau of Special Services and Information (BOSSI) or "The Red Squad" as some critics called it, the 1950's and early 1960's were the best of times, and the late 1960's and early 1970's were the worst of times. Challenged by a need reflected in an increasing number of street demonstrations, terrorist acts of sabotage, vicious internecine struggles within political groups, and the proliferation of radical, political organizations, Special Services grew into an effective intelligence operation rather naturally and unconsciously. In the 1960's, new aspects of social unrest and protest, reflected in the anti-Vietnam War movements, groups involved with racial equality, and student and women's groups, presented Special Services with problems with which it tried to cope.

An intelligence operation is simply a euphemism for spying. The word is anathema to us, and we pay a price for our indulgence. During World War II, secret codes were not broken, because "gentlemen do not read other people's mail," yet then and now police departments can be rendered impotent by our reluctance to entrust them with the development of intelligence gathering.

The Bureau of Special Services reached a high order of effectiveness in the late 1930's and early 1940's as it responded to the then potential dangers of World War II and the foreign sabotage and spying occurring in America. In the post-war period, the Bureau lapsed into ineffectualness due to the absence of the dangers of wartime.

The Cold War in the 1950's induced a period of growth of Special Services. The unit became very active in 1958 when it found itself increasingly challenged by the foment among exile groups, especially those from Latin America and Hungary. People within the New York City Police Department were receptive to expanding and intensifying the function of the Bureau, and successful arrests, based on intelligence gathered by the Bureau on street demonstrations by exiles, led to the use, once again, in 1961, of policemen and women as undercover agents assigned to penetrate groups who might be engaged in criminal activities.

Infiltration operations had been used effectively in the 1930's and 1940's against communists. The operations had focused on potential criminal behavior, with the inherent knowledge by the police that no criminal behavior might be uncovered. The question of target selection was extremely important, and generally the Bureau set out to intercept criminal acts that originated in known political philosophies.

By 1965 BOSSI had infiltrated a large number of subversive groups whose activities included the use of criminal means to achieve their ends and had participated in a sensational series of arrests. The Statue of Liberty case is only one example of a series of largely unreported interdictions of criminal acts. The agency also solved such cases as the bazooka attack on the United Nations and a Minutemen conspiracy. It investigated the right-wing activities of the American Nazi Party and the National Renaissance Party, the public bombings by Puerto Rican Nationalists, and plots by the Revolutionary Action Movement and the Black Panthers. Although reports of these cases were made available to the public, BOSSI's operations were little-known.

BOSSI wiretapped, infiltrated, bugged, photographed, surveyed, investigated, spied, and unashamedly undertook any strategy that enabled it to do its job effectively. The unit was kept under only one restraint: the Bureau had to obey the law punctiliously. At no time was any member of the unit permitted to engage in provocative or illegal acts, and it is a measure of the success of this restraint that the agency has never been successfully accused of overstepping legal limits. Every wiretap order was secured from the courts, and every infiltration had a crime as its target.

I came to the Bureau of Special Services as a detective in 1957 after having worked as a patrolman in the Red Hook section of Brooklyn and as a detective in the Youth Squad and precinct squads in Chelsea and Greenwich Village. Perhaps due in part to my knowledge of Spanish, I was assigned to investigate the disappearance of Jesus de Galindez, a Columbia University professor who had vanished in March 1956. I remained in Special Services, with a brief departure in 1958, through two promotions to sergeant and to lieutenant until my elevation to captain in December, 1965 when I received a field assignment. My interest in the unit resumed when I became an aide of Sanford Garelik in 1966 and continued into the 1970's when I commanded the Inspections Division, a unit similar to the Bureau.

By the mid-1960's, I felt that the Bureau was more effective than any other federal or state investigative unit. We were using our own carefully selected, undercover employees, and we had penetrated subversive groups more successfully than we ever anticipated. Lincoln Rockwell's close associate was our agent. Malcolm X's friend, whose jacket was perforated by a bullet when Malcolm was murdered and who *Life* photographed as he gave Malcolm mouth-to-mouth resuscitation, was our employee. Well-established functionaries in other groups were also our agents. When one group began to plot some political assassinations, BOSSI's infiltration was so effective that we were not only able to dismantle the plot and make arrests, but we also detected the conversion of one of our own agents to the group of plotters.

BOSSI had become a highly effective unit due mostly to the efforts of William Knapp. Sanford Garelik, who became the highest ranking uniformed officer in the Police Department under Mayor John V. Lindsay in 1966, had commanded the unit in the early 1960's. As virtually his first official act,

Garelik appointed Knapp as the new commander of BOSSI. As Garelik's aide, I had argued strongly for this appointment. Knapp's value to BOSSI had been amply demonstrated in the preceding years when, as a captain, he had tirelessly directed a series of complex intelligence operations with the unit. He was smart, tough, dedicated, willing to take risks, honorable, and respected. Under Knapp's leadership, the unit flourished.

However, at the very time when Knapp assumed command, the forces that brought him to that command were imperceptibly setting into motion the factors that would, once again, render BOSSI ineffective. As in most organizations, the fate of BOSSI lay in the hands of its commander. A few years after his appointment, Knapp prematurely retired because of a heart condition that we were all unaware of. Knapp's departure resulted in an inadvertent, and probably unsought, attenuation of the unit that its bitterest enemies had not been able to accomplish.

Before Knapp's resignation, the growing effectiveness of BOSSI inevitably heightened its visibility to the public. Although the unit avoided publicity—the full measure and scope of its activities are very far from known even today—the increasing number of public appearances by undercover agents before the courts to testify in criminal cases unavoidably led to exposure. Their undercover work and their testimony attracted the attention of critics who initiated a drumfire of opposition that grew louder proportionately with BOSSI effectiveness.

The election of a liberal mayor, John V. Lindsay, and his appointment of a tough-minded, liberal police commissioner, Patrick V. Murphy, created a political climate, reflecting a prevailing public attitude, that was not hospitable to the operations of an intelligence unit. Their resistance to BOSSI was instinctive and reflected an aversion for spying, particularly in political matters. Neither man had had any previous experience with BOSSI, and the unit was left alone to lapse into a period of decline, confusion, obscurity, and ineffectualness. The departure of Knapp was crucial. After him, a succession of inexperienced and unsympathetic commanders were appointed. Many had not worked within the unit previously, and their unfamiliarity with BOSSI freed them of any commitment to its goals.

It takes many months to develop an effective executive in the specialized and, to most policemen, totally unfamiliar field of investigation. That city administrators, already disaffected by BOSSI's undercover activities, appointed inexperienced commanders to the unit helped to hasten the decline of the Bureau.

During the late 1960's, a federal grant study resulted in the reorganization of the unit, undertaken by people who were unfamiliar with BOSSI and its history. The unit underwent another change of name that strangely symbolized its shifting identity. During this period, some BOSSI agents were permitted to receive CIA training in possible violation of CIA's charter that prohibits domestic operations. This illegal misstep, the first serious one in BOSSI's recent history, reflected the inexperience of executives who were not knowledgeable about BOSSI's mission.

BOSSI has gradually ceased to be an effective unit. Part of its work is now done by ad hoc task forces, designed to deal with problems of the moment like the Black Liberation Army's attacks on police, the Puerto Rican Nationalist bombings, and other acts of terrorism. These temporary task forces are not really prepared to assume a permanent responsibility for gathering intelligence, nor are they designed for that purpose. Task forces respond to fires, like the bombing of Fraunce's Tavern, by trying to put them out; BOSSI tried to intercept the arsonist before he lit his match.

The post-Watergate revelations of the questionable activities of the FBI and the CIA illustrate the dilemma facing anyone asked to pass judgment on the operations of an intelligence gathering agency. Shall people in a democracy remain passive to the assaults of subversives and terrorists, or should they risk the creation of an intelligence organization—federal or municipal—to meet that threat? Unlike subversives, terrorists introduce a new dimension into public disruptions, because they strike randomly, often killing innocent and unsuspecting people.

When I encountered a former BOSSI colleague just after the Fraunce's Tavern bombing on January 24, 1975 in New York City, he remarked that the explosion would probably not have occurred if BOSSI were operating as effectively as it once did. Although recognizing the fundamental unfairness of such a judgment, given the odds against infiltrating any single plot, I grudgingly tended to agree. I recalled a plot about five years earlier when a group intended to blow up police stations. Special Services had penetrated the conspiracy and was able to replace the dynamite in the plotters' bombs with a harmless powder.

Ten years ago, the bombers of Fraunce's Tavern would very likely have participated in picketings, distributed pamphlets, and prepared tracts. Some kind of public evidence would have been available, because a cause must be articulated and espoused. Converts to that cause must be made, and they are enlisted publicly through organization, speeches, pamphlets, and demonstrations. If the names and histories of the bombers did not appear in BOSSI's files in 1975, then I would conclude, not that the terrorists had effectively hidden their traces, but that the agency had failed to meet its responsibility to investigate potential subversion and criminal activity. Recidivism is more pronounced in political activities than in strictly criminal behavior. Predictably, the explosion at Fraunce's Tavern initiated the creation of another task force to cope with this threat to public safety. In the 1950's and 1960's, BOSSI would have considered the task force as an affront.

Recent years have witnessed the increasing willingness of dissident groups to employ terror to achieve their ends. The Irish Nationalists, the Puerto Rican Independents, the Palestine Liberation Organization, and groups like the Symbionese Liberation Army have demonstrated how vulnerable a complex and inter-related democratic society has become to attack; how ready many groups are to exploit this vulnerability, and how unprepared most countries are to cope with disruptions and terrorism.

People are conditionable through law. If some people are counterproductive or subversive within a larger society, then a deterrent can be sought to deflect them from terrorism and random killing. The deterrent can be positive or negative; it can take the form of rehabilitation as in probation, or it can be negative as in incarceration. Above all, the conditioning must be embodied in law. To deal with a deterrent usually takes the form of negative sanctions, but, before these can be applied, the criminal behavior and the criminal must be identified.

Critics of police intelligence have railed at the inclusion and identification of the names of innocent people in the files of an intelligence agency, as if this identification was, in and of itself, damaging to the person listed. A long, complex investigation will inevitably produce much data and a large number of names. An intelligence unit must evaluate each piece of information received and must systematically catalog it. The compilation of a dossier necessarily requires completeness and neutrality. Names of innocent people will reach the files of an investigative unit. Names of people with previous arrest and prison records may also be filed, and they are also presumed innocent of specific criminal activity until the police department, for which the investigative unit functions, makes an arrest. Under a municipal criminal justice system, the city prosecutor, working with the police department and the investigating unit, must prove in court that an alleged perpetrator is *not* innocent. That a name of an innocent person appears in the files of an investigative unit does not imply potential or real criminal activities. When a dossier is compiled for possible court trial, solid, incriminating evidence must be available to the prosecution, and it is the responsibility of the investigating agency to make sure that that evidence is complete and impartial.

That innocent people have been arrested is a danger in a democratic society. Some of these arrests are due to chance, but others may be due to careless investigative work. It is the responsibility of an intelligence unit to provide complete, objective information which should be as conclusive as possible. That innocent people have been arrested on such evidence is no proof of their guilt. Proof may or may not lie in a dossier and in the thoroughness of an investigation; guilt is determined only in the courtroom.

People in a free society are understandably reluctant to entrust much power in local, state, and federal governments. Fear of the abuse of power frequently causes a free society to curb its government's effectiveness yet an acquiescence to unchecked power is even more dangerous. We are left with a dilemma: we must safeguard our freedom and privacy through agencies that try to do just that, while making sure that all these agencies do not become a bureaucratic Big Brother that destroys our liberties.

I wrote this book to explore this dilemma, by describing the operations of one investigative organization, an intelligence unit of an urban police department. When I first wrote this study in 1968, my purpose was to counterbalance, from the view point of the police, the negative public opinion of investigative operations. Risks were involved to the agency through its exposure to the public and to myself for revealing some of its secrets. Commentary of the study was limited to a small group of friends, opponents, and rivals. A fair amount of interest in the work was reflected in the underground press prior to the discovery, on March 8, 1971, of the study by the New York *Times*. The interest of the *Times*, which carried a long account of the study, was unquestionably aroused by the secrecy surrounding all intelligence operations and the suspicion that such secrecy might conceal improper, if not illegal, activities.

My own views, tempered by the perspective of a decade of separation from BOSSI and reevaluated by necessity after the Watergate hearings, have changed. Although I had formerly resisted the need for accountability and controls in investigative work, I have come to realize that they are necessary. Rewriting my original study for publication has been a kind of semi-subliminal recognition of that need. It seems clear that a free people cannot risk total reliance on the good instincts, moral sense, and self-imposed restraints that an undercover agent or his commander is willing to impose upon himself. Some kind of monitoring group, representing the people, is needed. It should be a select committee of officials elected to a city council, a state legislature, or to Congress. Their responsibility would be to monitor the activities of an investigative unit to prevent abuses of power and to enforce its findings through recommendations to the principal municipal or state executive, or to the Congress.

In the 1960's, the overbearing effect of BOSSI's agents on demonstrating groups may or may not have inhibited the free exercise of constitutional rights, but if the police thwarted constitutional rights, then an abuse of power occurred. The existence of names of innocent people in an intelligence agency's file—even if they are never used in a damaging way and are kept as a part of the record to indicate innocence or non-involvement—involves an individual's right of privacy. Finally, the amount of power that a free society is willing to invest in its protectors is perhaps the most important matter for a democratic society to measure.

We all recognize the need to use spies and other legal, but distasteful methods to investigate police corruption and organized crime, but we instinctively bridle at the employment of spies in political and governmental areas. Somehow we must come to terms with our schizophrenic attitudes if we are to effectively combat terrorism and political corruption as well as organized crime and police corruption. Patty Hearst was not found until she had apparently participated in a bank robbery and until most of the Symbionese Liberation Army were dead. Her prolonged absence, as well as the occasional disappearance of people like James Hoffa, seem to indicate an underground of criminal activity and terrorism about which police intelligence units have little information.

When a bomb explodes, the public demands action, and newspapers editorialize self-righteously. When an intelligence operation is examined, critics generally argue against it, and its successes are conveniently forgotten. Critics should attack investigative agencies for exceeding their authority or violating rights and laws, but it is a dangerous emasculation of these agencies to render them powerless only because their power frightens us.

For law enforcement people intelligence requires, first, a heightened awareness of social forces, a kind of consciousness-raising to those social signals that alert police to potential crime. To police, much of that potential crime exists today in the urban ghetto. Dodge City served as the prototype of crime a century ago; today the South Bronx in New York City and the poverty areas in all major cities are frontiers of crime. The police are the front line of the forces that try to maintain peace and security there. They need great amounts of information on which to predicate their plans to maintain social order, and it is the function of the intelligence unit to furnish them with this data. When data is not supplied, a crisis like, for example, the one that gripped Israel during the Yom Kippur War of 1973 occurs.

A reactive or response model, which has police responding to events after they have occurred, keeps police in a Keystone chase after targets. A proactive model, which has the police obtaining data on possible future events, permits us to anticipate and intercept problems. Virtually every human act is predicated on intelligence, and advance information conditions our actions and reactions. The quantity and quality of advance information on a matter will determine the effectiveness and appropriateness of a response by police to that matter. An organization or a government without intelligence is blind and undirected, but an organization with intelligence is an alert and effective force—needing controls over its activities, over the technical centralization of its information, and over its employees.

People must begin asking themselves what kinds of organizations and government they need and want; to help begin making choices, I have in this book detailed the operations of one intelligence unit which, for awhile, was an effective law enforcement unit. At a time of post-Watergate disclosures that have tended to discredit investigative operations, I hope my study will demonstrate that such a unit can and did function within the law and that much of the recent discredit of investigation, must now be curbed.

CHAPTER II.

Mandate and History

Where Law ends, tyranny begins
—William Pitt, Earl of Chatham 1708-1778

The New York City Police Department operates under a broad but explicit mandate, expressed in the New York City Charter as follows:

> The police department and force shall have the power and it shall be their duty to preserve the public peace, prevent crime, detect and arrest offenders, suppress riots, mobs and insurrections, disperse unlawful or dangerous assemblages and assemblages which obstruct the free passage of public streets, sidewalks, parks and places; protect the rights of persons and property, guard the public health, preserve order at elections and all public meetings and assemblages; regulate, direct, control and restrict the movement of vehicular and pedestrian traffic for the facilitation of traffic and the convenience of the public as well as the proper protection of human life and health; remove all nuisances in the public streets, parks and places; arrest all street mendicants and beggars; provide proper police attendance at fires; inspect and observe all places of public amusement, all places of business having excise or other licenses to carry on any business; enforce and prevent the violation of all laws and ordinances in force in the city; and for these purposes to arrest all persons guilty of

violating any law or ordinance for the suppression or punishment of crimes or offenses. The commissioner shall make such rules and regulations for the conduct of pedestrian and vehicular traffic in the use of the public streets, squares and avenues as he may deem necessary which shall not become effective until filed with the city clerk and published in the City Record. The violation of such rules and regulations shall be triable by a city magistrate and punishable by not more than thirty days' imprisonment, or by a fine of not more than fifty dollars, or both. (1)

Every unit of the Department, every official act, and every plan must be related to the accomplishment of the basic missions described above. Any significant deviation from this bedrock mandate weakens the organizational edifice and threatens the success of the entire operation of the police.

The daily operations of the Department are made difficult and complex by the unique character of New York City itself. The city is a major port of entry and, as such, is host to thousands of people arriving by boat, car, and plane every year. Many stay and participate in the uniquely American process of assimilation known as the "melting pot." New York City is the core of a megalopolis comprised of some eighteen million people within the immediate environs, many of whom participate in the morning and evening commuting to and from the central city. New York is also host city to the United Nations and to over a hundred delegations that participate in its deliberations.

The city is a conglomeration of races, religions, nationalities, and cultures as well as a political center that has historically attracted the exiled. Within its borders are groups and individuals representing every shade of the political spectrum from farthest right to extremest left. New York City is the capital of many movements, and the richness of its diversity is matched only by the complexity of the labyrinthine paths the leaders of these movements take to realize their aims. The metropolis houses pacifists, fascists,

Peking-style as well as Moscow-oriented communists, Black Muslims (growing decidedly less oriented to race since the recent death of Elijah Muhammad) and Black Nationalists, anti-Castro as well as a few pro-Castro Cubans, Puerto Rican Nationalists, exiles from many Latin American and Eastern European countries, student groups of all persuasions, Minutemen, John Birchers, Nazis, civil rights groups who are militant-violent and non-violent, and many other organizations that at any given time may wittingly or unwittingly create a problem that police must solve.

The political and social foment that began in the 1960's has boiled with particular intensity in New York City. Without addressing itself to the underlying causes of social unrest or to the rightness or wrongness of any particular act, the New York City Police Department, as the agent of law enforcement and social order in the city, has had to contend with the acts resulting from social unrest and violations of law. Sit-ins, chain-ins, lie-ins, large demonstrations and even small picket lines may constitute disruptive acts that threaten the orderly functions of government. As such, they become a violation of law to which the police must respond. The objective function of the police is to enforce the law and to find a delicate balance between the right of demonstrators to dissent effectively and the rights of others to live and work peacefully and, if they wish, to respond to the dissent.

In addition to the problems created by political and social groups, New York is frequently faced with the prospect of assuring the safety of a visiting dignitary, a head of state, or even the President of the United States. Annually hundreds of these visits occur, and each represents problems peculiar to itself. In a city that hosts scores of Iranian students, many of whom are hostile to their government, a visit by the Shah of Iran represents security problems very different from those posed for example by a visit of the Emperor of Ethiopia, whose appearance may excite romantic musings but does not inspire much hostility. The responsibility for the safety of these eminent visitors lies with the New York City

Police Department, because it is the only organization with the manpower and materiel resources to assume such responsibility.

In evaluating the security techniques employed in safeguarding a U.S. President, the Warren Commission stressed the importance of obtaining advance intelligence information on persons or groups likely to constitute a threat to a visitor's safety. No policeman should forget that between 1956 and 1964, sixteen major political assassinations occurred throughout the world. (2) While political assassinations continue to be attempted, the killings at the Munich Olympics introduced the world to a new variation in radicalism and political expression: terrorism. Terrorism has been adopted and has spread with epidemic force, striking with terrifying unpredictability and effectiveness all over the world. Terrorists have discovered a new tool of political expression.

Any labor strike is a dislocation of public order. It stops an activity that presumably is useful or of service to the public. The degree of dislocation, however, varies with the size and nature of the labor dispute. The transit strike of 1966 constituted a true emergency for New York City. The movement of people required to keep the city functioning is essentially accomplished by efficient subways and buses. The termination of transportation service created personal and economic hardship for millions of people. The interruption of the supply of any essentials such as food, electricity, fuels, transportation, garbage removal, or health services create a crisis in a city's life. A police department must cope with the results of these crises to blunt the edge of the emergency. Once apprised of a potential problem, the magnitude of its impact, its probable duration, and alternative measures that can be taken to ease the public's burden, the police can view a crisis as having manageable proportions and can take steps to deal with its effects.

One of the most authoritative works on police administration, *Municipal Police Administration,* comments on the inability of police departments to cope with labor-management disorders:

> The police are in the best position to discharge the duties for which they are organized and equipped if they stay within the field of law enforcement. . . .It has been found sound police practice to maintain effective working relationships with both management and labor. The police must know and should have the confidence of responsible management representatives and labor leaders . . .The purpose of such meetings (police and management and labor) is to determine the background of the dispute so that an estimate may be made of its probable severity and duration. In such conferences the principals may be informed or reminded of the general responsibilities and limitations of the policies the police will pursue in the situation. Properly conducted, such conferences tend to reduce the inevitable frictions which accompany civil disturbances.(3)

Any police department in a large city must work with many different federal and state agencies in addition to scores of city offices involved in the day-to-day operations of city government. The very size and complexity of an urban police department dictates the existence of a coordinating unit to serve as liaison with these organizations and the department itself. This unit's role is to facilitate the flow of information, intelligence, and data. Its duties are as simple as notifying the Immigration Service of an alien's arrest and as complex as providing public safety for a publicly unpopular national leader.

Some of the problems besetting police departments as they attempt to maintain law and order are solved by the function of intelligence, the gathering of information for the purpose of accomplishing a mission. Intelligence has been defined as "all the things which should be known in advance of initiating a course of action."(4)

The New York City Police Department is the largest municipal police agency in the world, generally employing approximately thirty-two thousand people now described as police officers. Like the Cyclops Polyphemus, the New York City Police Department would be virtually helpless to cope with the many sudden, unexpected public crises without its eye: the police intelligence unit. Without the information provided by this unit, the Police Department would be engaged in an endless round of reactions to seemingly spontaneous crises and in coping, on an emergency basis, with rapidly developing incidents on the streets. Almost certainly such crises would increase if the police did not make proper preparations to anticipate them. The successful intelligence operation not only secures information but will also analyze and evaluate it in order to furnish the police with logical alternative plans for coping with future, potentially explosive events.

In the New York City Police Department, the intelligence function is assigned to the Bureau of Special Services. Its mission is to secure information relating to the political or social activities of any person or group, which are likely to result in a crime or a serious problem for the police. A branch of the Detective Division, this unit has traditionally been under the office and direction of the Chief of Detectives. In the manual of the Police Department, the unit's duties and responsibilities are to 1. investigate labor disputes, 2. guard visiting dignitaries, 3. cooperate with the United States Immigration and Naturalization Service, and 4. conduct other investigations as directed by the Chief of Detectives or other competent authority.

Police departments are semi-military organizations, established along authoritarian lines, charged with responsibility for maintaining the peace, granted the powers with which to discharge their responsibility, and operated on a rational system of priorities that permits the allocation of limited resources. The decision-makers in a department must be furnished with facts and the significance of the facts as well as with well-founded projections of intelligence data, if they are to make the desired number of correct decisions. Too many wrong decisions, based on ill-conceived options, are dangerously wasteful. As O. W. Wilson wrote, "the fundamental purposes of intelligence is to keep the chief informed."(5)

Few groups intent upon a breach of law will reveal their plans, and rare is the organization that will furnish even approximately accurate figures as to how many people will participate in a given event. Fewer still can properly assess the potential risks inherent in a demonstration as a result of the activities of groups opposing the demonstrators, and none will reveal the details of any illegal plans willingly. Despite this lack of information, a police department must know how many men to assign to a given event, what equipment to send, what precautions to take, whether policewomen or detectives will be needed, and what possible charges can be made in given situations. This knowledge together with other details constitute intelligence. A functioning intelligence unit will furnish a police department with an overview of the people the department is directed to protect so that necessary measures can be taken to insure the public's safety. In New York City, providing this overview to the Police Department is one of the functions of the Bureau of Special Services.

A recent survey of a large metropolitan police department stated:

> He (the chief) should also have information concerning the structure, membership and plans of secret organizations engaged in subversive activities. These may include groups that threaten the national or community safety and welfare. They will also include confederations created to inflame religious and racial prejudices and those that foment disturbances and violence.

Later the report recommended:

> An efficiently operated Intelligence Section should provide the Commissioner with information concerning the activities of organized criminals and subversive groups operating within the community.(6)

In examining the manner in which the intelligence gathering responsibilities of the Bureau of Special Services are met and to analyze the administration of the unit, it is useful to note again that the Police Department manual states that Special Services is "to conduct other investigations as directed..." In practice, this duty has evolved into the most important function of the unit: the investigation of subversive or potentially disruptive people or groups. Disruptive or subversive acts have long been defined by Special Services and the Police Department as being activities that either involve a breach of law or an occurrence that might impair the rights of the participants or others.

Very little information is available on the subject of the development of intelligence on a municipal level by a local police agency. The McCone report on the Los Angeles (Watts) riot of 1965 revealed that intelligence on the activities being used to sustain the momentum of the riot in Watts appears to have been minimal. Investigative experience has revealed that groups always exist within a ghetto area which have a vested interest in igniting and sustaining a disorder. The identities and activities of these people and groups must be known if the disorders they plan to create are to be prevented from becoming riots.

The Watts experience contrasts sharply with the Harlem riot of 1964. The death toll was one person in New York compared to 34 people in Los Angeles; 144 injured in New York compared to 1,032 in Los Angeles; 519 people arrested in New York compared to 1,032 in Los Angeles. Property damage amounted to approximately forty million dollars in

California whereas in Harlem 541 stores were damaged, and the extent of property loss was lower than in Watts. The Los Angeles riot started on August 11, 1965 and lasted until August 17; in New York the disorder lasted from July 18 to July 23. These and other statistics all indicate that the New York City experience was far milder than that of Watts, although other objective factors like population concentration would seem to predict a more severe result in New York. As we shall see, the less destructive experience in Harlem was due to the existence of superior intelligence which guided appropriate police action in New York.

O.W. Wilson, while Superintendent of the Chicago Police Department and one of the most influential writers on police administration, wrote:

> He (the Chief) should have similar information regarding those in his community who may be members of secret organizations that threaten the local or national security through subversive activity or espionage. He should know what organizations are devoted to engendering racial hatreds and disturbances and what their programs and plans are.(7)

The operations of an intelligence unit raise many policy questions, especially in a free society. The answers to these questions are vitally important to the welfare of the public which the unit serves. Strict adherence to concrete concepts is absolutely critical to the preservation of constitutional freedoms and democratic life. Terms like, "subversion," must be clearly defined and generally understood. In New York City, for example, subversion is synonymous with criminality; if an act is not a violation of law, the police should not be concerned with it.

J. Edgar Hoover, as Director of the Federal Bureau of Investigation, distinguished between dissent and subversion:

In the United States, the subversive is a law-breaker when he violates the law of the land, not because he disagrees with the party in power. And anyone who violates the law commits a criminal act even if the motives of the lawbreaker are self-servingly claimed to be political. If we ever permit political motives to justify lawbreaking, we shall develop political tyrannies in this country as similar instances have developed tyrannies in other countries.(8)

It may have been the instinct and philosophy reflected in these words that prompted Hoover to veto the notorious (and illegal) Huston Plan in the early days of Watergate. It is ironic that the legendary "enemy" of the left, Hoover should have become the champion of civil liberties in at least one notable incident in the early days of the Nixon administration.

Hazy ideas of a subjective nature are fatal to intelligence in that the ultimate cost of these ideas is the loss of public confidence and support. To investigate groups because they are "subversive" or because they practice "radicalism" or because they threaten "national security" leads the investigating unit to breaches of law that simply turn the unit into a criminal agency. Slavish adherence to outmoded but cherished shibboleths will not serve the police administrator well. The essence of a successful intelligence operation is objectivity.

Concerning the problem of affording security in a free society, the Warren Report commented:

Under our system, measures must be sought to afford security without impeding the President's performance of his many functions. The protection of the President must be thorough but inconspicuous to avoid even the suggestion of a garrison state. The rights of private individuals must not be infringed. If the protective job is well done, its performance will be evident only in the unexceptional fact of its success.(9)

The injunction in these words applies with equal force and relevance to the visit of any head of state.

The evolution of the Bureau of Special Services (BSS) into the unit primarily charged with securing, analyzing, evaluating, and transmitting data has been a gradual and almost organic one. The present organization was founded in October, 1912 as the Radical Bureau; its primary purpose was to investigate the status of foreign aliens. In 1915, it became the Neutrality Squad, directed to ferret out "bomb throwers, German agents, and anarchists." By 1921, the police were looking into Communist Party activities, and by 1923, the Neutrality Squad was renamed the Radical Squad.

Within the Radical Squad in 1924 were three sub-units: the Bomb Squad, the Industrial Squad; and the Gangster Squad. The labor investigative function developed during the industrial strife of the 1920's and 1930's, but the Gangster Squad, assigned primarily to inquire into the activities of criminal gangs, ultimately died with the end of Prohibition.

On January 1, 1931, the entire organization was renamed the Bureau of Criminal Alien Investigation, and on May 13, 1945, it was renamed the Public Relations Squad. This deliberate misnomer existed until April 15, 1946 when it became the Bureau of Special Services and Investigations (BOSSI), and this name was shortened to the Bureau of Special Services on August 1, 1955. The label, BOSSI, however, is still used to identify the Bureau.

Special Services successfully infiltrated the Communist Party during the 1930's and 1940's and contributed to the internal security of New York City through the discovery of many cells. World War II brought other dangers like bundists, fascists, and other extremist groups, but even then the "Trojan Horse" nature of the communist threat was not forgotten. The principal thrust of the Bureau's defense against communist activities was to interdict espionage and illegal courier operations.

The 1950's were a quiescent time, although former undercover agents were testifying before government committees and exposing communists well into the 1960's. There was little real activity in New York City of a threatening nature, and the Bureau settled into a rut of inactivity and disuse. The increasing interest and involvement of the FBI in the espionage area and in the communist field tended to restrict the operations of the Bureau.

The 1960's, however, burst with fury upon the city's life. Castro was in Cuba; Trujillo was in the Dominican Republic. The pacifist movement gained great momentum. Peking-oriented communists gave new militance and determination to the flaccid communist movement and posed new threats to the peace of the city. Black Nationalist groups assumed more menacing proportions. Groups that had been sporadically active during the 1950's, including Puerto Rican Nationalists, Nazis, and splinter groups of the far left and far right reemerged as the 1960's began. Groups like the John Birch Society, Students for a Democratic Society, and the Minutemen appeared and brought heated controversy into what already was a boiling potpourri of groups, thoughts, and movements. In addition to all these organizations came the civil rights revolution which, if it did nothing else, created a series of problems for the police that were unparalleled and unprecedented in law enforcement history.

All of these groups created police problems, relating to public peace and order, and the solution of these problems was the primary responsibility of the New York City Police Department.

The Rules and Procedures (R&P) of the Police Department are notably cryptic concerning the activities of the Bureau of Special Services. The few references made, in addition to the functions enumerated at the beginning of this chapter, are interesting, because their very vagueness has permitted an evolutionary development that enabled the

Bureau to acclimate to rapidly changing political and social forces. Chapters seven and nine of the Rules and Procedures make three references to the mechanics of notifying the Bureau when an alien is arrested. Chapter nine, paragraph 49.9d reveals that the Bureau should be notified of any arrest for a "communistic disturbance" and paragraph 89.0 directs that notification of the Bureau be made if there is an "arrest or seizure in connection with distribution of anarchistic or other unlawful literature . . ." Chapter two, paragraph 39.6 states:

> Members of the force shall promptly notify their commanding officer of any suspected espionage, sabotage or other subversive activities. The Commanding Officer shall send a report in duplicate in a sealed envelope to Bureau of Special Services and, when the matter is urgent, shall first telephone the information.

These three statements are the only references in R&P to the Bureau. The nebulousness of the directives is vaguely reminiscent of Christ's injunction to Peter: "Thou art Peter, and upon this rock I will build my church."

The civil rights movement brought to New York City violence and non-violence; support and opposition; militancy and passivity; petition and demand; legality and illegality; unity and diffusion; purpose and chaos; progress and backlash. It was already a changing society. Many paths were and are being taken toward the goal of equality that all fair-minded people acknowledge to be the legitimate aim of blacks and other minorities. Some believe that the end—social justice—justifies any means taken toward its realization. Others hold that the means temper, condition, and alter the end and that the methods used are as important as the objective. The former group has created many problems for law enforcement agencies, and the anticipation and resolution of these problems have invariably fallen to intelligence units.

One of the grim results of the civil rights movement were the urban riots that characterized life in the 1960's. Racial revolt had not occurred since the days following World War I when black bitterness and white resentment led to "at least twenty-five race riots of record."(10) The disorders of the 1960's resembled those earlier race riots. The McCone Report (11) reveals a pattern of disorder, violence, pillage, burning and chaos in Watts that was to be repeated again and again in American cities. Descriptions in this report could easily apply to any of the major cities touched by violence during the summers of 1964, 1965, and 1966.

Police administrators could not have been expected to cope with such complex events without intelligence data. An effective intelligence unit must not only furnish information during an event, but must also be able to prognosticate further possible outbreaks of violence on the basis of an isolated incident and its effect on a community. Predicting potential violence can only occur within an informed, alert intelligence organization closely attuned to the activities within its community.

Inevitably the question arises whether a municipal unit like the Bureau of Special Services parallels or duplicates the functions of the FBI, the Secret Service, or other federal agencies. These agencies are essentially concerned with the enforcement of federal laws which are predicated on interstate activities. Theirs is a national responsibility that does not permit encroachment on the preserves of local government. The federal agencies, in addition, rarely possess the resources necessary to do a thorough job in any given locality precisely because of the limitations on their mandate in any one city. The fact that the Secret Service constituted less than five percent of the total force guarding President Kennedy in Dallas (12) illustrates, in a graphic, unmistakable way, just how real federal limitations in a city can be. State law enforcement agencies, on the other hand, are totally removed from both federal and municipal agencies, because they prefer to engage in highway patrol and related operations.

No local law enforcement agency can duplicate the functions of federal agencies. In New York City, federal agencies and Special Services have coordinated their efforts so that the goals of both can be realized. Their cooperation has been particularly evident in narcotics, counterfeiting, kidnapping, and recently in the innovative organized crime task force.

The essential duties performed by Special Services are to guard visiting dignitaries, which is an operational as well as a staff function in practice; to investigate labor disputes to permit the Police Department to cope with strikes; to cooperate with the U.S. Immigration and Naturalization Service in investigating the status of aliens; to investigate subversive activities as well as other inquires, and to serve as liaison with federal, state, and local agencies in all of these matters. All these activities are interrelated. An analysis of the functioning of an intelligence unit within a major metropolitan police department will illustrate how these activities are interrelated.

CHAPTER III.

Administration and Personnel

An intelligence unit has a very limited clientele. It is axiomatic that the entire intelligence effort is undertaken simply to keep top police management informed and aware of their options. Again and again, it is said that a "unit must become the eyes and ears of the Chief of Police." (1) Since the Bureau of Special Services rarely undertakes operational responsibility, it has been spared the necessity of justifying a special project. For example, the operational involvement of the Central Intelligence Agency in the Bay of Pigs "invasion" is generally regarded as being a prime cause of the venture's failure. Faced with the prospect of a large-scale assault, CIA found itself promoting those bits of intelligence that justified the assault and deemphasizing those factors that seemed to indicate failure. The temptation to an intelligence unit of becoming involved with operations must be resisted. The intelligence gathering enterprise is undermined when the collecting unit acts on the information it gathers.(2)

In the late 1960's, the Bureau of Special Services under the Chief of Detectives, was a branch of the Detective Division of the New York City Police Department. All members of Special Services belonged to the Detective Division and were a part of the quota of the Division. The commanding officer, usually of inspectorial rank (the equivalent of a major or colonel) administers a unit that has captains, lieutenants, sergeants, and approximately sixty male and female detectives permanently assigned to overt operations. The occurrence of an emergency or the pursuit of a special project may occasionally double this number, but only for a short time. W. Cleon Skousen has stated that "an intelligence unit should never involve more than one percent of the personnel."(3) The complement of Special Services is less than a fourth of one percent of the entire force. An active rate of attrition, caused by promotions, deaths, transfers, and other separations, generally keeps the number lower than the quota.

The first thing that impresses an observer is the fluid nature of Special Services. The unit is not, in any sense, compartmentalized. It has, instead, retained a remarkable flexibility that permits it to change the focus of its attention with dramatic speed and effectiveness. Members are encouraged to broaden and deepen their knowledge through assignment and training, but the essential use of the unit's men and women as interchangeable professionals is kept uppermost in administrators' minds. While a detective may be regularly assigned to labor disputes, background investigations, subversive affairs, or analysis, evaluation, or documentation, the use of this detective on other matters, as need arises, is common practice. The flexible use of a professional person develops a specialist *and* generalist with a fixed continuing responsibility, who has a genuine appreciation of the objectives of the unit and of his contribution to it. That a detective may be receiving conflicting or contradictory orders from two or more superiors is one of the prices paid for administrative flexibility. Observation has repeatedly demonstrated that the violation of the principles of chain of command is a commonplace of the Bureau. The focus of the unit's attention can be changed so often and over such a wide field that compartmentalization would lead to paralysis.

The commander oversees the entire operation, makes all final decisions within the unit, selects the projects that will be pursued, dictates policy, and generally determines the direction and strength of the organization's thrust. Whatever may be said in principle and theory about the dispensability of people, the harsh realities of practice have taught the New York City Police Department that the quality of the commander is critical to the success of the Bureau. The commander is the central figure who guides the unit. The quality of the leadership largely determines the efficacy of the Bureau. It is no accident that two commanders of Special Services during the recent past have risen to Chief Inspector, the highest rank in the force.(4)

The commanding officer of the Bureau should keep the broad outline of policy clearly in mind. The commander must consider as prime factors of that policy the following: 1. The intelligence gathered must be transmitted to top management in intelligible form; 2. The intelligence obtained must be presented in an honest and forthright fashion. No reluctance, inhibition, or hesitation to pass bad news upward to the commander can be allowed; 3. The intelligence should be related to the legitimate objectives of the department. Its direct relevance to the police department's mission is essential; 4. The intelligence has to have a sound basis in fact. No fanciful theories, no favorite ideas, and no hazy concepts should be forwarded through the chain of command. The unit is not a sounding board for anyone's personal theories; 5. The intelligence should be analyzed, interpreted, and evaluated on a logical basis. Inferences and deductions must be labeled as such; and 6. The intelligence should be presented in a usable form. Implications of the data should be described fully, alternatives should be indicated, and options as to possible action should be described. The function of analysis is an integral part of the intelligence-gathering process.

The commander has to restrict the activities of his unit to areas in which it is competent and keep its activities within the guidelines of the unit's mandate. Experience and the unanimously held belief of police administrators indicates that the commander has direct and immediate access to the leading executives of the police department: in New York City, the Police Commissioner, the Chief Inspector, the

Chief of Detectives, and the Chief of Patrol. A necessary concomittant of this access is the confidence in which the commander and the unit should be held by these four men. O.W. Wilson wrote:

> The intelligence unit should be headed by a man in whom the Chief has complete confidence. If for any reason it is impossible to obtain such a man, it is better not to have such a unit.(5)

A captain serves as executive officer of the Bureau. As such, he participates in every phase of the operation and keeps the administration of the unit functioning smoothly. His presence insures command continuity in the absence of the commander, and he frees the commander from the burden of administrative chores so that he may give his time and attention to policy, planning, and strategy. The executive officer frequently directs special projects and serves as an understudy, advisor, and aide to the commanding officer. The fact that the Bureau works twenty-four hours a day makes the executive officer's availability essential. Late night decisions are frequently required, and the commander or his deputy should be on call at any given hour of the day or night.

One lieutenant oversees clandestine or covert operations like those, for example, that resulted in the arrests of people conspiring to blow up the Statue of Liberty, the Minutemen who conspired to plan attacks on leftists, and members of the Revolutionary Action Movement (RAM)(6). Actual arrests and related operational responsibilities are delegated to other units of the Police Department, because arrests are not a function of the intelligence unit.

Although written thirty-one years ago, an account describing covert operations of the Bureau retains an unmistakable timelessness. The nature of undercover operations has not materially changed over the years. The targets for infiltration may have changed, but the tactics employed remain much the same:

Since the undercover unit of Special Squad #1 was formed in June 1940, twenty-eight detectives and policewomen from this squad have joined the Communist Party. Not only did these operators have to surmount the barriers mentioned in 'Under Cover' but in addition each had a skeleton in his closet that rattled—they were members of the New York City Police Force.

Earl Browder (once a well known member of the American Communist Party) wrote: 'One of the most effective weapons in the hands of the enemy is the agent-provocateur, the stool-pigeon, the spy in the ranks of the vanguard of the proletariat—the Communist Party.' First on Browder's list of 'human rats' are those 'planted in the party . . .by the Police Department.'

In more detail, Browder described what he believed were the duties of the Police 'stool pigeon.' They have the task of gathering information about the party and the individual members. They work diligently, attend every meeting, and take responsible assignments in the organization. They strive to be promoted to higher positions in order to get more important information to the Police Department, or to their bosses. They are very inquisitive about individuals, their names and addresses; they always like to get some inside 'dope' from and about higher committees. They are present in every possible place they can get into. They try to get hold of documents and keep them for a day or so. They try to find ways and means of getting to other party organizations and factions than their own.'(7)

Browder's understandable pique accurately describes some of the functions of the undercover operator.

Browder also describes, ironically, his own activities

when he describes the activities of a "stool pigeon" of the police. Like an infiltrator, he was diligent. He *was* the most faithful attender of meetings; he paid his dues, subscribed to the Party newspaper, and walked picket lines. His interest was constant and continuous. While others dawdled or drifted, he concentrated and performed. The challenge to BOSSI was to keep Browder and others like him from rising to policy-making levels within an organization or to initiate provocative public acts.

When I was associated with BOSSI, our relations with the FBI were extremely close, and I can recall kidding an FBI agent over the expulsion of a particularly dedicated and effective Communist Party member for "anti-Party" activities. I suggested that a cabal of FBI infiltrators had sought to weaken the Party by expelling one of its more effective leaders. When he smiled, I suggested that perhaps the Party would disappear if we both withdrew our infiltrators. The FBI agent winced at this heresy.

Our relations with the CIA were much more distant, with two exceptions. The confusion surrounding the hectic Bay of Pigs "invasion" thrust BOSSI into the middle of a blur of security activity with the Revolutionary Council that CIA hoped to install in Cuba as Castro's successors. BOSSI was asked to engage in some hectic errands to and from restaurants, hotels, and airports prior to the failure of the Cuban misadventure. The second major involvement with the CIA was similarly unsuccessful: the possibly illegal and certainly ill-advised training of BOSSI personnel by the CIA in the early 1970's.

The daily overt operations of the unit are supervised by other lieutenants; these operations include undertaking special projects, performing general supervisory duties, and generally seeing to the efficient functioning of the unit. An important special project in the 1960's was the annual organization of a special summer unit used to obtain information on ghetto riots and similar disorders. This unit, composed of personnel who operated on a semi-undercover basis, infiltrated mobs and street groups to determine who the leaders were and what plans were being made.

Many people who have been determined to instigate a riot have been discreetly removed from crowds and effectively neutralized as a result of these investigators. During the July 23-25 East Harlem disorders in 1967, members of this Special Services group were observing street conditions and people who were inciting crowds to riot. The inciters were later identified and arrested. Much of the potential danger of this developing riot was defused by the removal of these leaders from the scene.

The decline of street riots as a summer phenomena of ghettos illustrates that the disaffected soon learn the consequences of rioting. Not only were people injured and neighborhoods burned during a disorder, but, following the riot, burned out marginal businesses did not reopen, and residents had to leave their neighborhoods to get milk, cigarettes, and newspapers. A night of protest and looting were not worth the inconveniences that followed. The disaffected of the ghetto are, however, still disaffected, but they are expressing their grievances differently, more selectively, and purposefully, since the rioting of the 1960's.

The personnel who are closest to the daily, overt operations of Special Services are five sergeants who are first line supervisors; each has general responsibility for a specific area. Yet like the detectives, each sergeant has a role which remains flexible. Although one sergeant may oversee reports, internal administration, and clerical assignments, another, labor activities, a third, political organization, and others, security details, it is widely accepted and commonly understood that an immediate responsibility may involve their overseeing an operation quite outside the scope of their general supervisory duties.

The unit recruits its supervisors from the ranks of its members who have been promoted to sergeant. Although initial difficulties occur when former colleagues begin supervising their former peers, these problems are overcome in practice by the repeated necessity for issuing orders and the gradual acceptance of these orders by subordinates. The leadership potential of these sergeants is one of the critical factors considered in deciding to return them to the unit or not.

A serious objection to the practice of returning to the unit former detectives, who have been promoted to sergeant and tranferred elsewhere, is the administrative and organizational in-breeding that results when they are reassigned to the unit as supervisors. Fresh and vital approaches furnished by new personnel come from the highest and lowest levels of the unit. Special Services has not, within the past ten years, been commanded by a person who had any previous direct experience with it, and detectives are invariably newcomers. Although they cannot be considered new personnel, returning sergeants have the knowledge and experience to function effectively from the first day they begin doing their job again. They provide a continuity and consistency to the operations of the unit and need no costly break-in period. The very nature of the work is so unlike general police business that new entrants usually require extensive training, supervision, and orientation before they function effectively. When a good detective, who has been observed, evaluated, and tested, is promoted to sergeant, his accumulated knowledge and experience make the candidate a natural choice for return to Special Services as a supervisor.

The two most important factors accounting for the success of the operation are the choice of commander and the care and skill used in selecting recruits for Special Services. The first determines the quality of the leadership, the integrity of the unit, the imagination and daring of the enterprise, and the effectiveness of the entire operation. The second determines the quality of the people who must do the work.

Assignment to the Bureau of Special Services constitutes, for a police officer, entrance into the most prestigious unit of the Police Department. The intangible of prestige is buttressed by the appeal of promotion, especially since the ranks of

Detective 3rd, 2nd, and 1st grade have been eliminated to create a unit-wide egalitarian Detective 3rd grade, with a pay increase of between fifteen and twenty percent. The work creates no problems for the police officer; the need for the unit is clearly understood; its mission is unequivocal. No moral dilemma is posed as in the enforcement of gambling laws, and the patrolman's ordinary treadmill of investigation, report, arrest, and court testimony is avoided. The work is interesting, stimulating, challenging, and varied.

The Bureau of Special Services has as its recruitment base approximately 32,000 male and female members of the Police Department, most of whom would be delighted to be accepted by the Bureau. The recent computerization of the skills and attainments of police has made part of the selection process easier and more efficient. Vacancies in the unit occur at about the rate of six to ten annually. It is generally agreed, but seldom realized, that vacancies should be filled as they occur, for the unit needs an adequate supply of well-trained, experienced employees. The recruitment base, however, is not as broad as it would appear, because entrants are selected from a fairly narrow personnel band.

The unpredictable nature of intelligence work resulted in a felicitous representation of minorities within BOSSI's ranks. The existence of Latin American organizations, Puerto Rican Nationalists, and Cuban exile groups in New York City insured a heavy representation of Hispanics in BOSSI. The activities of the left, of the radical pacifists, and of the more militant of the hippie world provided women with jobs with Special Services long before the advent of Women's Liberation. Many women distinguished themselves in investigative work. The black revolutionaries also provided blacks with employment opportunities in BOSSI. The unit, in general, offered minorities job chances that were not generally available elsewhere.

The qualifications required for entrance into Special Services are sufficiently objective to permit any policeman or woman to conduct a self-analysis to determine their chances of selection. The qualifications have the virtue of eliminating suspicions of favoritism or deception in the selection process. Nothing is more destructive of morale than the suspicion that politics, friendship, nepotism, or dishonesty have played a role in entrance selection.

Selection factors are equally regarded and do not exclusively determine admission to BOSSI. For example, when a specific talent such as an unusual language ability may be needed by the unit, the possession of this skill may result in a police officer's acceptance. A fair preponderance of the following qualities is, however, generally required of the successful aspirant:

1. Good department record. A candidate should have exhibited a willingness to work, as demonstrated by his record of arrests, citations, letters of commendation, sick record, and a clear disciplinary file. The personnel folder of the candidate, which is comprised of a thorough biographical sketch of his official life and a comprehensive resume of his life before entering the Police Department, is invaluable in evaluating a candidate's suitability as reflected in records.

2. Education. BOSSI generally seeks college graduates, because the nature of the reporting and evaluation process requires a disciplined and sophisticated mentality that is able to define subtleties in perceptions and to transmit data in intelligible form. The guiding principle is that "the quality of police service will not significantly improve until higher educational requirements are established for its personnel."(8)

3. Intelligence Quotient. The Police Academy's Personnel Testing Unit administers a seventy-five question, thirty minute OTIS I.Q. test which has a possible high score of 133. The unit generally requires a score of at least 110 on this test which measures verbal, numerical, and abstract visualization abilities.

4. Language ability. The unit's work makes knowledge of foreign languages essential. Strong preference is given to candidates who know widely used languages like Spanish, French, Italian, and German.

5. Technical skill. Expertise in some aspect of investigative technology is an important requisite of an investigative unit. A candidate should possess some photographic and electronic skills in the field of communications. Sensitive and complex investigations may require the use of court-authorized wiretaps, and an aggressive unit does not flinch at finding people experienced with wiretapping.

6. Recommendation of a candidate's commanding officer. The comprehensive personal evaluation by a commander is an invaluable guide to a candidate's intangible and immeasurable qualities which must be known. Attitude, initiative, motivation, integrity, sobriety, and other personal characteristics are rarely documented in a police officer's record. The commander's personal observation of a candidate over a long period of time therefore constitutes an information source that must be considered.

7. Personal interview. An interview is another test of intangibles and should be used to complete the candidate's record. It is undertaken only after the rest of the investigation is completed. Questions are designed to measure the candidate against his credentials and background, to reveal any flaws in both, and to answer any questions that the investigation may have raised. Although it is well known that interviewing requires great skill, it also requires thorough preparation and advance information about a candidate.

8. Professionalism. Finally, a candidate should be an experienced and able police professional with approximately three to ten years of service and should be between twenty-five and forty years of age. More than normally curious about the world, the candidate should be solidly motivated toward intelligence work.

Unlike BOSSI, the Central Intelligence Agency generally recruits its new investigators from college graduates of eastern universities. Accepting recruits from the top ten percent of the senior class, the CIA observes potential candidates during their last year and attempts to evaluate their personalities. Of every hundred applicants, approximately eighty are rejected immediately because of inadequate education or poor background. The remaining twenty are investigated, and eleven are found to talk too much, drink excessively, have relatives in communist-oriented countries, or are security risks. Applicants are given lie detector tests primarily designed to detect homosexuals and others who might divulge information under duress. Candidates are tested by the Princeton University Educational Testing Service to find specialists such as lawyers, physicists, linguists, etc.(9)

Because of the growing interest in human rights, many governmental agencies are being legally challenged concerning employment rights. During a recent lecture at the FBI National Academy in Virginia, I was asked my opinion on the employment of homosexuals in police work. Before depriving any group of people of their right to work in law enforcement, police need to have evidence based on research on which to base such a deprivation. No evidence exists, or has been developed, that proves that homosexuals should be deprived of their employment rights in law enforcement. Lacking that evidence, I would refuse to deprive homosexuals as well as any other minority of their right to work. It was an unlikely question in an unlikely place, and the reaction to my answer was surprise. The question, having been asked, needed to be answered.

A recent article described the following qualities as being essential to success in intelligence work in a metropolitan police department: personal and professional integrity, loyalty, discipline, professional competency, creativity, prudence, education, orientation (awareness of environment), and dedication.(10) The qualities reveal a thread of consistency that is woven throughout the intelligence apparatus at all levels of government. The requisites are much the same whether an intelligence organization operates on a national or local level. Whatever the level, only candidates of the highest quality are to be recruited for intelligence work.

The Bureau of Special Services is a magnet that attracts

many worthy candidates, as well as the unworthy. The possibility of favoritism, of placing a friend or relative in this organization is a very real one. In past years, it was not unthinkable that the well-connected but unqualified frequently found their way into BOSSI ranks. The process of enlisting influence to obtain such a transfer would be phrased, in police jargon, as "having a hook" or "having a rabbi who can put in a contract for the unit."

To prevent favoritism and administrative corruption, two practices are followed. First, the careful selection of a commanding officer, who will not permit dishonesty, should be made, and second, objective standards for entrants should be established. Any interested candidate can easily compare his background to the requirements of the unit. If he feels qualified, he is entirely correct in seeking an explanation of his rejection, and in practice, he invariably obtains the particulars that affect an unfavorable decision about him.

The "merit system provides that government personnel shall be selected, retained, and promoted on the basis of its capacity and demonstrated ability to advance the purposes of government."(11) This statement guides Special Services today in its personnel decisions.

Candidates for Special Services are recruited in many of the following ways: 1. U.F. 57 process. Used throughout the Police Department, this form is available to any policeman who can use it to request a transfer to any unit, listing his reasons for the request and his qualifications. The use of this form has been an especially successful administrative maneuver, and its salutary effect on the morale of the Department is incalculable. 2. Elite units. Highly trained police units other than Special Services attract superior candidates who have gained experience under trying conditions almost daily. The Tactical Patrol Unit, composed of volunteers who work from six p.m. to two a.m. in high crime areas, is one such unit. Selecting candidates from special units not only secures superior candidates, but also motivates those remaining in elite units to redouble their work efforts.

3. Screening by the Personnel Records Unit. This unit has computerized the skills and attributes of members of the Department, and its computers can produce, within minutes, lists of candidates who possess qualifications required by Special Services. 4. Members of the Detective Division. People who have demonstrated an affinity for intelligence work are a natural source for Special Services personnel.

Ideally, the Bureau would like to attract an experienced young patrol officer, who is a college graduate with a foreign language ability and with an I.Q. of approximately 120, who is a good, clear writer with an appreciation of political subtleties, and who has energy, perserverance, dedication, loyalty, and is willing to work. Surprisingly, many candidates approximate this prototype, and the caliber of the personnel in Special Services is definitely superior to the rest of the police population.

Once admitted into the unit, a patrolman faces a training process which progresses gradually from simple tasks to more difficult assignments. Every operation of the unit has been analyzed in an instructional volume, which trainees study to learn the nature of intelligence work and the procedures used to achieve objectives. The volume is a ready reference work to which trainees frequently refer during early training. During the first few months, trainees are paired with experienced Special Services people. On-the-job training is heavily supplemented with frequent instructions from various superiors, memorandums from the commanding officer, and staff conferences held for orientation and instruction.

Generally, a year is required to develop an investigator who can perform most tasks of the unit with acceptable skill. Developing experts in various specialized areas takes substantially more time. A serious personnel problem of the unit is the heavy promotional attrition that results from attracting superior candidates. The typical entrant has little difficulty in passing promotion tests for sergeant, and rapid promotions cause a steady drain of experienced personnel.

However, when these men are promoted and transferred to patrol assignments in uniform, they make the patrolmen under them much more conscious of the nature of intelligence, and as a result, the patrolmen frequently learn from their mentors more sophisticated and technical ways to gather intelligence.

The sergeant's examination, open to all police, is going to be passed more readily by the typical Special Services detective than by his less qualified counterpart elsewhere in the Department. A detective's return to uniformed patrol as a sergeant—a long-standing policy of the New York City Police Department—tends to reenforce among the patrol forces the value of intelligence gathering and the transmission of information.

Allen Dulles said on the training of the intelligence officer:

> It (the training school) will also give courses on the substance of intelligence itself, how intelligence services work, how information is analyzed, how reports are written etc. But the guts of such training is the practiced business of field operations.(12)

Similar to that given on a national level, the intelligence training of a police officer in New York City is a combination of the academic and the practical.

During an apprenticeship period of approximately eighteen months, a trainee is still a police officer working with a white shield. Once he has demonstrated his worth through his performance on the job, he gets the coveted gold detective's shield and becomes a Detective 3rd grade with a substantial pay increase. From his first day to his eventual last day, he is subject to constant observation which is summarized in an annual evaluation. This formal process determines his retention, demotion, or promotion in the unit.

The process of evaluation requires that a rating of "Outstanding, "Above Average," "Average," "Unsatisfactory," or "Not Observed," be given to the following traits: judgment, job knowledge, dependability, job attitude, relations with people, manner (military bearing, oral expression, etc.), and overall evaluation. Blank spaces for name, ranks, shield number, special duty, sick time, and period observed appear on the same side of the form. The reverse has space where a comprehensive paragraph must be written appraising the man, his achievements, his progress as well as his value to the unit. The most difficult evaluation is a forced ranking scale on which every patrolman being observed must be rated "first," "second," "third," etc. of the total number observed.

In practice, each officer rates all men and women and submits recommendations to the commanding officer who then schedules a conference of all superior officers to discuss and determine, in the give and take of a lively discussion, a final, formal list of evaluations. This list is submitted to the Chief of Detectives. The discussion tends to overcome personality problems, prejudice, or other predilections to bias that so frequently intrude into the evaluation process. The final evaluation is available to any man or woman who seeks to learn their status, and those who are ranked low are advised of their standing.

The sine qua non of the evaluation process is the fair mindedness of those who evaluate and judge. Without impartiality, no amount of control will make justice possible; with it, no control is really needed.

The great value of these annual appraisals is the reflection of the status of the unit and its personnel that the superior officers are forced to undertake. Neither the volume of work nor the distractions of the moment can be allowed to divert attention from these appraisals. The professional future of employees is determined by these evaluations. Decisions concerning promotions, retentions, demotions and transfers are made during evaluations, and opportunities to reward outstanding performances and to terminate the employment of the unfit are faced.

The alert evaluating officer must be aware of the attraction of safe, general responses that do not lead to either the promotion or demotion of people but do result in complacent satisfaction. An aim of the evaluation process is to reduce the number of poor performers in the unit in order to raise the future level of acceptable performance.

The success of the intelligence operation is predicated on the quality of its personnel. Allen Dulles said, "The most serious occupational hazard we have in the intelligence field, the one that causes more mistakes than any foreign deception or intrigue, is prejudice."(13) The elimination of the potentially prejudiced, as well as the complacent, is one of the vital functions of the evaluation process. To make the evaluations vital, tough-minded candor is essential.

The Bureau of Special Services has ready access to the people who administer the Police Department. Internally, the organization follows the classical pyramid. The principles of unity of command and span of control are, admittedly, frequently violated, due to the spontaneous and creative nature of the work. Imagination, insight, and flexibility cannot be bridled to administrative principles. The Bureau recognizes the value of having one man give directions to another, who learns from this exchange just what is expected of him and to whom he must report. The principle of unity of command must occasionally be sacrificed to the imperatives of an immediate case. Additionally, one superior may sometimes find himself directing more men than he can effectively control. This, too, can be tolerated, because the men themselves are trained to operate on their own initiative and are granted the widest operational latitude, once they have proved they can handle complex assignments. The span of control is widened by the subordinate's initiative, resourcefulness, and self-reliance.

Special Services engages in approximately a thousand fairly extensive investigations each year that fall within three general areas; labor investigations, security assignments and subversive inquiries. Approximately six hundred additional communications are received each year that require thorough investigation. Of these, a perennial chestnut is a letter that identifies a German recluse as the Nazi, Martin Bormann. Any elderly German male who speaks with an accent and lives alone is prey to the accusation that he is Martin Bormann. Even this allegation is faithfully investigated.

The administrative controls developed by the Bureau of Special Services over the years have the virtue of simplicity and the undeniable quality of utility. Controls have developed, grown, been discarded or retained solely on the basis of their value to the organization. The Bureau is not saddled by any rigid procedural controls that would require mindless adherence to outdated methods simply because higher authority required them.

The usual Police Department records, relating largely to the organizational life of the Bureau's members, are kept by the Bureau. Time, payroll, service, disciplinary, personnel, and similar records are maintained as required, but the daily life of the Bureau revolves around a twenty-four hour log. The log is comprised of a running account of every significant event affecting the unit, a diary of events listing every meeting or activity of interest, schedules of expiring labor contracts, arrivals and itineraries of visiting dignitaries, and details of announced or discovered picketing and other demonstrations. This log outlines the work to be done and forms the basis for personnel assignments.

Frequently, two or more investigators will be reporting on the same event without knowing of the other's involvement. Just as frequently, two or more undercover infiltrators, unaware of the true status of each other, will be reporting on an activity. Because these reports are carefully monitored, it was discovered that one Special Services member had been converted to the revolutionary cause he was investigating. He furnished the Bureau with false reports that were being refuted by two other agents. The man was then given a specific assignment, and it was reported that he had not completed it although he reported that he had finished the assignment. The converted revolutionary was quickly forced to resign from the Department.

As important as the twenty-four hour log is the maintenance of a file of written accounts of orders, decisions, and policies that may have been made orally. The policies of an intelligence unit should be made a part of the unit's record and should be available for review. If intelligence agencies are to be held accountable for their activities, documentation of these activities must exist. During the hearings of the Senate Select Committee on Intelligence, Richard Helms, the former director of the CIA, testified that he had given oral orders, upon instruction by the President, to destroy a stockpile of deadly poison. Helms did not discover for years that his orders had been contravened and that no written record of his directive existed to be shown to the Committee. If intelligence agencies are to be permitted to instigate covert operations, they must be able to prove to a democratic society that they have not acted illegally or autonomously. Accurate and complete records are their primary defense.

Once a detective has been assigned to a case, it is given a number, based on the nature of the job, and an investigation is conducted to obtain all pertinent information. Allen Dulles has said, "Yet it is a fact that about eighty percent of all information. . .is obtained openly."(14) The detective has to find the material that is readily available and cull the germane data from sources like newspapers, books, organizational literature, etc. One of the first things an intelligence officer learns is that information is readily available. Once the officer's consciousness is raised and his objectives are defined, the investigation of his case is simplified.

A preliminary report is submitted to the first line supervisor who examines it for completeness, directs follow-up action, and discusses the matter with the executive officer or lieutenant on duty. Naturally, reports of some urgency are immediately telephoned to the Operations Center of the New York City Police Department as well as to the Bureau of

Special Services. If the case should be brought to the attention of the top administrators, a formal report is prepared and forwarded. This report is in the nature of a narrative that addresses itself to the problem of who, what, where, why, how, and when.

Whether or not a report is forwarded to headquarters, the data it contains must be documented. Entries of future events are made in the diary, and the names of people or organizations listed are documented and filed for future reference. These listings and documentations are filed in a huge bank of raw data available for use in evaluating the character and purpose of any active organization or person. The files of the Bureau are almost entirely comprised of these references that once totalled approximately one million cards.

This huge data bank has been the source of many problems and endless litigation. The specter of maintaining a "file of subversives" has caused the Bureau to decimate this bank of information to a minuscule. The debate as to whether the existence of such a file is socially useful was resolved before the discussion reached any level of sophistication. A simple resolution of a complex issue was reached: the records were expunged, and the right to privacy prevailed.

The reports relate to matters as diverse as the security needs of foreign missions, installations, and people; the itinerary and anticipated problems concerning the arrival of a dignitary; reports of meetings; analyses of past, present, or future demonstrations; an evaluation of a labor dispute; the background of an individual or organization; or any other investigation by the Bureau that relates to the business of the Police Department.

Every investigation produces at least two results for the unit: an evaluation of an immediate problem and its ramifications and, secondly, data for the files for possible future reference. The overt sources of information constitute a mass of data, the very size of which poses the greatest problem for the collector. Discriminating between the useful and the merely interesting can be very difficult. A recent book related that the CIA collects 200,000 newspapers, books, and magazines each month, and information from the material is recorded on punch cards. The agency was alleged to have forty million cards by 1964.(15)

CHAPTER IV.

Subversion

Knowledge is power.

—Francis Bacon

The use of knowledge, information, or intelligence can silence and defeat a mayoral candidate, or it can immobilize an activist attorney. It can help elected politicans and their appointees to remain in office, and it can help them to keep others out of office. It can even reassure the office-holders of their virtue as the sins of others are confirmed by hard evidence. A local or national administration can cloak itself with a self-righteous mantle of morality under which any action may be pursued.

An effective intelligence agency is a powerful instrument for the protection of society or for the private use of political office-holders and administrators. Powerful men will want to use a strong agency for their private purposes, and secrecy, a frequent necessity, can be extended on flimsy pretexts to conceal corrupt practices. It is almost axiomatic that secrecy will breed grotesque distortions of behavior and activity while openness and inquiry will help an intelligence agency to fulfill its proper mission.

The Watergate disclosures and related investigations of the FBI, CIA, IRS, and other governmental agencies have placed the problem in precise focus, but a resolution of the problem, as always, is not simple. The protection of a democratic society requires the existence of effective intelligence agencies. Democracy and the freedom it allows require that the agencies of the government remain responsive to the will of the people. That responsiveness is usually achieved through a system of checks and balances that keeps the major branches of government in contention and more or less under constant surveillance and question. If any area of the operations of any governmental branch is spared scrutiny, then that area is ripest for abuse. Watergate has shown that a democracy cannot afford privileged sanctuaries of inquiry.

The Bureau of Special Services, accountable to the hierarchy of the New York City Police Department, was at all times an instrument of possible abuse. Subjected to no independent audits, accountable to no outside agency for its operations, overseen by no one, the Bureau could have undertaken any inquiry into any area of activity. It is easily conceivable that an ambitious police executive could curry favor with a mayor by giving him politically valuable information on friends and foes. It is more than conceivable that the FBI under J. Edgar Hoover engaged in abusive practices, and it is now certain that the CIA engaged in illegal activities.

All of these powerful intelligence agencies can be employed positively or negatively. The challenge to a democratic society is to make intelligence agencies effective representatives of the nation's laws and of the people.

That the enforcement of laws and the safety of the people of New York City is the responsibility of the Police Department can require the Department to be involved in activities as varied as preventing a petty theft with the presence of a foot patrolman to the interdicting of a complicated plot to assassinate Civil Rights leaders by an extremist group. The Police Department relies not only on the deterring effect of an omnipresent uniformed officer but also upon information garnered by its intelligence apparatus.

The Bureau of Special Services is charged with gathering and compiling intelligence on subversive activities and transmitting to the Police Department data on people and groups who, because of their plans, are likely to create problems requiring police attention. This charge is the most important responsibility of the Bureau; it requires the greatest expenditure of time and effort; it determines finally the success or failure of the enterprise.

Subversion is generally defined as an effort to overthrow or destroy government through illegal means. As with most words that contain an emotional charge, this one has been used so often that its true meaning has been all but obliterated. Nothing is more dangerous than to permit hazy concepts of subversion to arise and control policy, for then witch hunts are certain to follow. The Bureau of Special Services applies the synonym of criminality to subversion; if an act is not a crime, then it is not subversive. This definition gives the word concrete form and provides an investigation with a definite focus.

The New York State Penal Code is concerned with many crimes that cover the specific acts of subversive groups. They include anarchy, conspiracy, riot, assault, disorderly conduct, and many others. Weapons statues also play an important role in these acts.

Contemporary American society harbors many different political groups who seek to overturn the government or fragment it. The Nation of Islam or Black Muslims seek reparations from the United States for three hundred years of slave labor and call for the establishment of a separate black state somewhere within the country. The recent liberalization of the Black Muslims becomes all the more remarkable for its contrast with the Muslims' racist history of enmity toward the "blue-eyed devil." Probably motivated by such forces as the popularization of the moslem religion—especially by black athletes—Wallace Muhammad, upon succeeding his father, Elijah, made the surprising announcement, in the summer of 1975, that the Nation would no longer exclude whites. A basic change in the philosophy of an organization like Wallace Muhammad's must alert an intelligence officer to the existence of social forces that may remove a group from the ranks of subversive organizations and classify it as a legitimate religious entity. It is early to judge the ultimate direction the Black Muslims will take, but

1975 marked an abrupt philosophical change of direction of the group.

The American Nazi Party, although small and ineffective, seeks to establish a fascist state and to eliminate "Jewish traitors." Ironically, the Bureau of Special Services became a champion of free speech when the Party was active. Although its philosophy was anathema to us, we all felt strongly that we were also the guardians and guarantors of constitutional rights of free speech. The history of the Bureau is replete with references to its championing the rights of dissidents to be heard, and, during the early 1960's, Lincoln Rockwell, the head of the American Nazi Party, asked for a permit to speak at Union Square. The issue of free speech was never more clearly drawn. At first, the Civil Liberties Union fought for Rockwell's right to speak but, it seemed to me, abandoned him under the pressure of critics who successfully kept him from speaking. I fought hard on this issue and felt that its defeat had done violence to the Constitution. The issue dropped from public consideration, and Rockwell never spoke in New York City.

The Progressive Labor Movement calls for "smashing the state," killing police and judges, and organizing a "people's militia" to realize the goals of this Peking-oriented communist organization. The Nationalist Party of Puerto Rico has engaged in acts of violence throughout its history to promote independence for that island. Militant black groups have actively promoted racial hatred and engaged in violence. Other organizations like the Minutemen have not hesitated to break laws in attempting to be heard. These and other groups of similar illegal persuasion are the legitimate concerns of any police department. The only effective surveillance is provided by an alert intelligence unit.

In addition to the blatantly subversive, other groups, individuals, and movements require surveillance by police. The pacifist movement rapidly expanded in seeking an end to the involvement of the United States in Vietnam. In pursuing their policies, pacifists engaged in mass meetings, marches, parades, picketings, sit-ins, civil disobedience, and occasional deliberate violations of law to force a confrontation with authority.

The student movement, as a result of decided pacifist tendencies coupled with determined interventionism in the administration of schools, created problems for law enforcement agencies. Students resorted to deliberate violations of law, characterized mainly by obstructing the functioning of their schools, to state their objectives. Their acts ultimately became the concerns of police.

Policing student activities, a particularly sensitive area of police operations, cannot be abdicated because of spurious considerations of academic freedom. A campus is not inviolate from legitimate police inquiry, and crimes like assault or destruction of property must be investigated in the same way as crimes occurring in other public places. Addison H. Fording wrote:

> If a police agency which may be faced with a major campus disturbance is to be forewarned and properly prepared, it is essential that personnel be assigned to maintain a continuous observation of campus activities. The identity and background of student organizers should be known, since it may well provide a clue as to the action which can be anticipated. Rallies and meetings should be attended and published material carefully studied.(1)

The Civil Rights Movement was comprised of people who represented many varied points of view as to what means were to be used to effect social change. Nevertheless, even the most pacifistic groups within the Movement resorted to sit-ins, chain-ins, lie-ins, and other forms of civil disobedience to demonstrate publicly their goals. It is important here to distinguish between the committed citizen who engages in civil disobedience as a protest, and who openly accepts the possible consequences of disrupting the public peace, and the criminal—like a terrorist or a murderer who strikes alone and who has no intention of confronting society. The former citizen is expressing an act of conscience to engage other citizens in debate, while the latter attempts to gain his ends through terror and intimidation. People working in law enforcement must learn always to distinguish between these two kinds of acts as they did in the 1960's when urban summer riots came to be understood as civil disobedience and protest.

In addition to groups in major movements, many good-sized groups, exiled from their respective countries, demonstrate in New York City and often break laws. Discussing all of these groups, W. Cleon Skousen wrote:

> Recent outbreaks of civil disturbances and insurrections have only highlighted the widespread need in some areas for solid, well-trained officers in thehecialized field of collecting intelligence data.(2)

Today, any intelligence unit must deal with the contagious effects of the philosophy and activities of movement groups. A result of the social and political foment of the 1960's is the increasing involvement of middle-class groups violating the law to achieve their goals. In New York City, a stall-in was organized by residents in Queens in October 1967, who blocked the entrances and exits of John F. Kennedy Airport to complain of the noise caused by jets flying overhead. A few weeks later residents of the Sheepshead Bay area of Brooklyn blocked traffic to dramatize their demand that a low-income housing project not be errected in their neighborhood. A similar housing controversy in Forest Hills in Queens further illustrated the frustration of middle-class people and their increasing willingness to act militantly.

These demonstrations, engaging as they did the one element thought to be the rock of stability in American society—the middle class—very dramatically illustrate the contagious nature of the disease of resorting to lawlessness to achieve a group objective. Recently, middle class citizens have closed fire stations by picketing to protest cutbacks in firefighting personnel, and when sanitation personnel were reduced, people ignited piles of garbage in the street to increase the number of garbage pick-ups in their neighborhoods.

Police agencies are frequently confronted with the dilemma of a good cause being supported through breaches of law. Like the problems of the middle class, the international plight of Jews in Russia may be addressed by chain-ins at the United Nations or harassing Soviet officials at their embassy. The virtue of a cause cannot blind a police agency to the need for information upon which to respond to what are, ultimately, disruptive public acts.

A police department must have the information continuously at hand to cope with the problems posed by the activities of disruptive groups. The delicate balances necessary for the functioning of a democratic society of checks and balances can easily be damaged by the irresponsible actions of a wilful faction. A democratic society is vulnerable to attack, and this very vulnerability is what tempts assaults.

OVERT OPERATIONS

Contrary to popular belief, the compilation of intelligence data is essentially a prosaic, unromantic process. Allen Dulles frequently stated that most intelligence information is freely available in newspapers, books, official reports, and on radio and television programs. To deal with all this information, trained personnel must be developed who are able to determine what intelligence is useful.

An important intelligence consideration is the selection of targets, i.e., who or what is to be observed. Selection is made particularly sensitive by the ramifications of a public disclosure of error. If an innocent person or organization were subjected to official scrutiny, the disclosure of error would result in embarrassment for the police and intensified attack by people interested in eroding public confidence in the police. Attacks against police are made most of the time, but their effect is weakened by the absence of concrete data upon which to base the charges.

The small but active organizations who seek to discredit local or national government will frequently focus upon the police, the most visible and attackable symbol of government. In a real sense the police are engaged in a battle for the minds and hearts of the public, especially in the ghettos. There, the revolutionary rhetoric centers on "the oppressor"—the police—as the hated symbol of an exploitive system. Rhetoric is fleshed out with charges of "police brutality" and spying by the "fascist pigs." Any shred of evidence that supports these charges enlists more converts to a revolutionary cause. The police have to be extremely careful to avoid lending any credibility to these charges and to repudiate with evidence, those same charges as soon as they are made. The public has a right to know and the government has an inescapable responsibility to inform.

Viewed from a narrow perspective, modern times, especially since the invention of the press and the computer, may be seen as an age of information. Learned tracts are published on every conceivable subject; pamphleteers busily distribute their wares; doctoral candidates write on the most esoteric subjects; television scrutinizes and analyzes a bewildering array of problems; newspapers summarize and quickly distribute information. We are continuously bombarded with reams of data, and we unconsciously develop selective sensory filters that help us delete extraneous information as well as help us to retain what is useful.

It is an age when more aspects of life become officially documented. We are identified by digits, credentials, licenses, credit cards, medical bracelets, and historical records of our activities from birth to death. By the time a young person of twenty-five is ready to enter a police department, a dossier can be compiled that contains sixty exhibits relating to that person's schooling, employment, military service, driving history, criminal antecedents, family history, and social and political affiliations. The sources from which a police dossier is compiled are mines of information for the alert intelligence agency, for those sources may be used again to compile dossiers on young subversive activists and terrorists.

When an array of data is matched to the inevitable necessity of attracting adherents to a radical cause, the investigative direction is determined for an intelligence unit. A subversive organization must grow in numbers if it is to grow in strength and influence, and growth cannot occur without attracting new activists. If the aims of a group are too extreme, then they may be muted or compromised, but goals cannot be completely changed, or the organization will be unwittingly attracting ideological adversaries into its ranks.

An organization must have a program, leadership (although several ingenious stratagems, notably the "cell system," have been employed to circumvent administrative leadership), meetings, literature, and the other accoutrements of organizational life because of their utility, convenience, and value. Once a person or an organization has aroused enough suspicion to warrant an inquiry, a background investigation is conducted. The selection of the target by the intelligence unit's commander, or a high ranking police official, is a sensitive choice. The criteria for selection are ill-defined, and judgments are usually subjective. One commander's target may be another commander's cause. The choice of a target has rightly developed into one of the really controversial problems of intelligence operations. Although no solutions exist, law enforcement professionals can begin to approach the problem by asking: Who selects the targets? On what basis are they selected? How thorough should the investigative penetration be? At what point should it be discontinued? How chilling is the effect of such surveillance on personal privacy and on the exercise of political expression?

When a group is the target of investigation, an inquiry will begin by determining the character of the organization. Is it a corporation with public stock, with members, or with religious affiliations? Is it operated under a trade name? The answers to these and other questions can be obtained from the office of the County Clerk where the principal place of business is on file. The laws of New York State offer definite advantages to the corporate structure, and incorporation is widely used to establish an organization's legal existence. On the Certificate of Incorporation is the name of the corporation, its officers, and its purpose.

This basic information can then be explored through credit rating agencies for information on the principals, the credit status of the organization, and the type of premises occupied. Utility companies are also valuable sources of information and enable the investigator to visit the location of the organization. Licensing agencies and other branches of government can be consulted when relevant. This early, basic phase of an inquiry is concerned with accumulating the recorded history of an organization, and all promising leads, which differ in practically every case, should be pursued to their sources.

When a person is being investigated, the individual's record can be determined through agencies that recorded birth, education, marriage, employment, military service, criminal history, credit rating, voting history, and residence locations. Each individual case will point in a distinctive direction, but at the beginning of an inquiry, all available information should be gathered. Later redundant material may be deleted. The ready availability of all this data on organizations and individuals makes an intelligence agency a tempting tool for unscrupulous politicians. The secrecy of the operations, the contacts developed, and the sources used all add to the attractiveness of using the unit for political purposes.

Intelligence operatives know from experience that a thorough inquiry into almost anyone's background will reveal damaging facts. The existence of these facts —and an agency that can discover them —can prove to be a temptation to ambitious police and politicians. Yet to make a thorough inquiry, an intelligence agency is rarely restrained by moral considerations; it has a case to investigate through, to a satisfactory completion. Egil Krogh's question, "Is it right?"—as he belatedly remembered the moral imperatives behind executive acts—has often seemed an obstacle to successful intelligence gathering. Although it has no moral mandate, an intelligence unit must avoid the possibility of allowing its intelligence to be used illegally, and Congressional investigations of the CIA and FBI have helped to determine instances when illegal abuses of intelligence have occurred.

Ironically, an individual's record almost invariably contains background information that would alert any security agency. The most successful spies of this century, Richard Sorge, Burgess and McLean,(3) all had references in their dossiers that indicated that they were very poor security risks. Sorge had references to youthful left-wing activity in the Gestapo files when he was spying for the Russians in the German Embassy in Tokyo. His case poses the classical dilemma for a free society: what is a security risk, and to what degree should a person's past be held against him? Sorge was able to give Stalin the two most vital pieces of information the Russian leader required: the approximate date of Germany's attack on Russia and the fact that Japan would not participate in that attack. The latter fact permitted the Russians to shift their Siberian armies to the European front.

Once recorded data are obtained, an investigation then focuses on the activities of an organization. Meetings are attended; picket lines observed; literature collected; activities watched. All observations are recorded. Placards on picket signs frequently become the clearest indication of the goals of an organization. A picket line, usually limited to communicating its message with shouts and chants, faces the problem of communicating its purpose to the general public. Picket signs—brief, clear, and striking messages—must state the reason for the demonstration and, as a natural consequence, the purposes of the organization. "Free Soviet Jewry," "Independence for Puerto Rico," and "Down with the Pigs" are, or have become, messages of unmistakable clarity and, for police, identifications of groups being investigated. The true leaders of an organization can also be detected at demonstrations from observing the behavior of the participants. Relationships within the organization and identities can be deduced from noting automobile license plate numbers on cars delivering people to join the group.

Overt operations will not elicit secret data or generally result in information that exposes criminal behavior. However, overt inquiries, usually undertaken by detectives, reveal plans for future meetings, picketings, and other demonstrations that may require the attention of police. Of central concern is the necessity of keeping police management informed of future demonstrations so that allocations of manpower can be made on a rational basis. Overt surveillance also provides promising leads for follow-up by undercover operations.

W. Cleon Skousen (4) described the function of an intelligence unit's protection of society as involving knowledge of: 1. subversive groups with the identity and background of their leaders, 2. problems of minority groups and where channels of liaison might best be developed, 3. procedures necessary for V.I.P. security, 4. current labor and management problems, and 5. the latest activities of special interest groups likely to become involved in civil disturbances or riots. Mr. Skousen adds that an intelligence unit should collect, correlate, interpret, and distribute information. Moreover, the unit must keep the Chief of Police informed of its activities, for as George P. McManus has said, "The Chief cannot know too much about the community, and he dare not know too little."(5)

COVERT OPERATIONS

The covert operations of an intelligence unit are those undertaken in secrecy and anonymity. These activities invariably get agencies into trouble and frequently result in the worst public images of police. The law, however, is the touchstone which should effectively prevent the abuse of secrecy. Covert operations are tempting to use, and few restraints exist to curb them. In using secret investigations, an agency must exert an almost religious adherence to the law. The intelligence unit is frequently tempted to think of the results to be obtained by investigation rather than the rightness of the methods used. However tempting the objective, e.g., the interruption of a criminal plot and the arrests of the plotters, the intelligence officer must subordinate objectives to the primacy of the law. Failure to subordinate objectives to the rule of law is the mistake that most often damages an intelligence agency.

Secret operations are generally obnoxious to citizens in a democracy. Bitter antagonisms are engendered when it is discovered that the inquiries have taken the unit beyond legal limits. Recently, for example, the Central Intelligence Agency gave aid to some student groups of promote "favorable" campus activity. The agency appears to have exceeded the mandate Congress gave it to limit its investigations to matters outside the United States. The appearance of excess was enough to generate enough Congressional opposition to cancel these domestic activities. Further, the action impaired the future integrity of the CIA by eroding public confidence in it.

David Wise and Thomas B. Ross wrote:

> The secret intelligence machinery of the government can never be totally reconciled with the traditions of free republic....the solution lies not in dismantling this machinery but in bringing it under greater control. The resultant danger of exposure

is far less than the danger of secret power. If we err
as a society, let it be on the side of control.(6)

Nevertheless, the police of necessity must sometimes engage in covert investigative operations, in so far as the law
allows, if the objective of community safety is to be even
partly realized. For example, society cannot be left to the
mercy of terrorist predators who strike at will to cause
havoc, misery, and death.

Covert operations include the use of informants, undercover police agents, surveillance techniques, and the use of
technical investigative equipment like "bugs" and
wiretaps.(7) Many police agencies use "inside" informants
who are in a position to reveal the developments within an
organization. Using informants, like every other investigative stratagem, has its virtues and its drawbacks. Informants
do furnish data coming directly from the target, with few
risks for the agency, since the informant is not officially
connected to the government. Informers are relatively inex-
pensive and easy to control. However, because a paid informant is generally under economic pressure to furnish information, he may fabricate some data to keep money flowing
to him. A conscientious informer frequently loses his en-
thusiasm after he evaluates the risks and experiences the
boredom of the assignment. The possibility also exists that
an informant may be "planted" to deliberately mislead an
intelligence agency. Frequently the use in an organization of
two or more informants, unknown to each other to be furnishing data, serves as a verifying control. No matter who
furnishes information, it must always be subjected to the test
of verification.

Undercover police agents are social and political chame-
leons, selected precisely because they are able to blend
naturally into the background of an area or group. They
assume new identities to conform to the specifics of the
target group, and gradually they insinuate themselves into
the confidence of the organization. Propinquity becomes a

major stratagem of the undercover informer. That he is readily available, willing to help, and ready to undertake arduous or unpleasant tasks for the infiltrated group quickly endears him to the group's leaders. To the informer, time cannot be viewed as the objective passage of minutes or days but rather as a function of the memory of an organization's leader. An agent may spend many hours on a group's work over a period of only six months, but frequently group members will come to accept, by a process of memory osmosis, the idea that he has always been there.

Great care must be taken to protect the undercover agent. An intelligence unit must assume that eventually a thorough-going inquiry of possible infiltrators will be undertaken by the target group. As a matter of fact, the more dangerous the target group the greater the care taken in checking new members of the group. To the informant, contact with the intelligence unit must be available to him at all hours of the day and night. The control or contact at the unit must guide and advise the agent through the entire investigative assignment.

An undercover agent lives, breathes, talks, eats, and sleeps his assignment. The fewer the social relationships he has the better. What made Ray Wood such an outstanding agent in the Statue of Liberty case was his lack of familial ties, his being from out of town, and his ability to devote himself totally and exclusively to his job. His knowledge of the jargon and workings of the New York City Police Department was minimal, while his commitment to the assignment was total. No police records were available on him when his case was resolved. All police matters relating to his investigation, appointment, and career had been centrally kept by the officer in charge of the Statute of Liberty case. No member of the Police Department could have discovered that Wood was a city employee. He had never set foot in any official police installation during the first months of his career except as a prisoner to be booked!

The undercover operation must be seen as a separate and

distinct area of police work, requiring its own administrative and organizational machinery, plant, and procedures. The agents are informational sponges, carefully absorbing data coming within their purview and gradually working themselves deeper into their target areas to develop access to increasingly sensitive information. Even the identities of other police officers within the same target area cannot be revealed to these agents. By not identifying agents to one another, the investigative unit safeguards its necessity to verify their informers' reports.

An undercover agent must be given a cover story that creates for him a new identity including a new name, birthplace, family, educational background, identification documents, and employment records.(8) An undercover man or, since they are frequently employed, woman, is an extremely valuable investigative operative because his or her activities can be manipulated. As a salaried employee and as a motivated, dedicated police officer, the agent can be ordered from one group to another and from one activity to another. The agent's investigative work can be guided and directed from hour to hour if necessary. Because undercover agents are police officers, their loyalty and responsiveness generally are far more assured than that of informants.

The investigative endeavor must be an organic process. Data gathered must be useful, germane, and accurate. Each stratagem is employed not only for the information it can elicit but also to verify the accuracy of material already contributed by other investigators.

Surveillance can involve observation of a location to determine how it is being used and who frequents it. People might be followed to determine their activities, and people, places, and things may be photographed for evaluation and analysis. Surveillance also includes recording license plate numbers of vehicles, rummaging through garbage cans for bits of discarded information, or simply mingling with a group to overhear conversations.

Surveillance is usually defined as a continuous observation of an individual or an area to detect developments, movements, or activities. It is as old as history itself. Even the Old Testament records that Moses sent men "to spy out the land of Canaan," and they returned after forty days to report to Moses, Aaron, and "to all the congregation of the children of Israel."

Although spying is an old activity, its techniques have been greatly enhanced by technological progress. The development of photography and the discovery of electricity provided investigators with an array of new devices. Minature listening devices have also increased the sophistication of spying. Today there exists a bewildering variety of electronic spying gadgets which are perhaps best symbolized by the transmitting "olive" in a martini or more recently, by tape recorders in the White House. As technology produces increasingly effective machines for spying, law enforcement personnel may be tempted, in using the machines, to exceed legal boundaries. The greatest restraint must be imposed by the law and by law enforcement officers in the use of these machines for spying or even simply recording information.

Wiretapping has been called the "single most valuable and effective weapon in the arsenal of law enforcement,"(9) and the President's National Crime Commission endorsed the use of wirtaps and "bugs". All supporters of wiretapping and bugging, including the Commission, invariably couple the demand for legalizing the use of wiretapping with the imposition of strict legal controls for its operation. Yet wiretapping, as well as tape recording, has been discredited because law enforcement agencies abused its use. Investigative administrators have not learned that ends, however noble, cannot justify illegal means. An Attorney General's claim that he can wiretap in "national security" cases, without authorization or judicial review, undermines public confidence in electronic surveillance. His later conviction of a crime, and his obvious misuse of power, should alert all law enforcement personnel that the use of electronic surveillance devices is an extremely sensitive, legal area of investigation.

Every investigation of consequence tests the mettle and resourcefulness of the investigators. An arsenal of resources—tactics and skills as well as technological devices—are available to investigators. Wiretapping—the interception of telephonic communications—is a useful investigative weapon when used legally. It is a truism of police work that even the most careful conspirators have careless moments on the telephone. It requires iron discipline to participate in phone conversations and avoid incriminating remarks. Sooner or later, even when a tap is suspected, a moment will occur when useful information is inadvertently revealed to the alert listener.

President Nixon, knowing that his office was bugged, could not maintain his guard and was eventually driven from office by tapes he knew were recording his comments. It is remarkable that he was unguarded enough to incriminate himself, yet an experienced investigator would have predicted inadvertent self-incrimination.

New York State requires that a court order be secured from a justice of the Supreme Court before wiretapping can begin. The order is requested by a District Attorney or Attorney General and is in effect for a maximum of thirty days (although it can be renewed). The granting of the order is predicated on a set of explicit facts that must convince the judge that evidence of crime will be elicited through wiretapping. The penalties for illegal wiretapping, which is a felony in New York State, are severe. The wiretapping equipment is centrally kept and secured to preclude improper use, and installations are directed from one major office that will undertake wiretapping only under court order. The controls over electronic surveillance, which have evolved over the years, are now reflected in the "Eavesdropping Warrants" section of the Criminal Procedure Law. They are so stringent that they make wiretapping practically useless in the one area of investigation—organized crime—in which it has been successfully employed.

Although evidence secured through wiretaps is rarely, if ever, used in court, this material nevertheless becomes an indispensable part of an investigation, leading to the discovery of other conspirators, fresh evidence, and new leads. Under Section 605 of the Federal Communications Commission, it is a violation of federal law to divulge to anyone the contents of a telephonic communication.

Generally, the same principles that control wiretapping apply to bugging, which is electronic eavesdropping on conversations. The Supreme Court has held that recording conversations with "bugs" constitutes a trespass and cannot be used as evidence. Most law enforcement officials support the President's Crime Commission's position that wiretapping and "bugging" should be permitted legally.

The investigation of subversive activities is largely a process of penetrating a criminal political conspiracy. Experience and logic have demonstrated that even with informants, undercover agents, surveillance techniques, and electronic devices as its basic means, investigating subversion is still one of the most difficult tasks of an intelligence unit. In New York City, the Bureau of Special Services encountered many such difficult jobs.

When the Knapp Commission undertook an aggressive investigation into police corruption, it learned how sensitive a covert investigation can be. It was the theory of the Commission that police corruption was a thoroughly developed system that required deep and determined probing—and a systematic prescription—rather than the identification and isolation of separate cases of corruption.

Taking a cue from BOSSI's previous intelligence experience, the Commission planted "field associates" in police ranks to spy on police activities and to report serious breaches of discipline or law. Policemen caught acting illegally were "turned around" when they were urged to cooperate to uncover further corruption. The police went into businesses of all kinds to discover what our own employees might be doing to or with them. Agents got their names on "pads"—lists of businesses and people who regularly pay off police for protection—to discover who was receiving money illegally. Agents would turn wallets containing money in to police officers to test integrity. Other "self-initiated investigations" were devised and employed as strategies that were unprecedented in that they pitted police officers against police officers. Although a wide variety of positive training programs were undertaken to secure rank and file assistance and cooperation with the Commission, using the methods of BOSSI to uncover police subversives was demoralizing to most members of the Department; undercover investigators who were independent of the Department should probably have been used by the Commission instead of turning police against one another.

BAZOOKA ATTACK AT THE UNITED NATIONS

On December 11, 1964, a bazooka shell exploded in the East River, while a group of anti-Castro Cuban exiles picketed the United Nations building to protest the presence of Ernesto "Che" Guevara in New York. The shell fell several hundred feet short of the United Nations building and did not injure anyone or damage property. The resulting public reaction, however, was tremendous due to the sensational nature of the attack and the daring of the planners. The incident became an international *cause célèbre*, especially to those who wanted to move the United Nations out of the United States on the pretext that its security could not be guaranteed.

The source of the attack was quickly traced to the Long Island City edge of the river where a bazooka-launching mechanism was discovered. No other clues, however, existed, and the investigators had to focus immediately on likely suspects if they were to determine who had fired the bazooka. The Bureau had been investigating the activities of

Cuban exiles for at least six years, and an impressive reservoir of information had been amassed both in the files and in the minds of people assigned to cover Cubans.

Immediately upon receipt of the news of the attack, the Bureau assigned detectives to assist the detectives in Long Island City who had primary responsibility for the investigation of the attack. Scanning the field of logical suspects, the BOSSI detectives quickly focused on anti-Castro Cuban exiles as probable suspects. Their deduction was further refined by concentrating on the militant elements within the Cuban group who would be capable of plotting a startling, military-like attack.

Suspicion finally centered on members of an exile group who had repeatedly demonstrated their fanatical opposition to the Castro regime and their readiness to damage the regime in any way they could. On the basis of information supplied by sources who had long been cultivated by Special Services detectives, three Cubans were arrested on December 22, 1964, exactly eleven days after the attack.

The Cubans—Julio Carlos Perez and two brothers, Ignacio and Guillermo Novo—intended to blunt the publicity of Guevara's speech before the United Nations on December 11. They were charged with possession of explosives and the intent to use them maliciously. Confessions were obtained, and they were indicted. However, the indictments were dismissed on June 9, 1965 by Supreme Court Justice J. Irwin Shapiro on the grounds that the confessions had been obtained illegally because the accused had been denied access to their lawyer. It was felt that the rest of the evidence in the indictment was not sufficient to prove the charge.

Despite the disposition of the case, some good public relations resulted from the affair. The quick solution of the case stilled those who sought to remove the United Nations from the United States. To the world, this case revealed a nation applying its laws even to presumed friends who violated the law to attack a presumed enemy, Guevara. The case also advised Cubans that violations of law would not be ignored. Finally, the investigation of the affair demonstrated that New York City had a police organization that worked efficiently and effectively to support the law and public safety.

An ironic footnote to the case is the fact that a principal investigator of the bazooka attack and the detective responsible for breaking the case was John Caulfield. Caulfield, who had worked for several years in Cuban affairs at BOSSI, became an aide of John Ehrlichman and was responsible for bringing James McCord into the Nixon re-election campaign as a security advisor. Caulfield also brought another key investigator, Anthony Ulasewicz, from BOSSI to Washington. Ulasewicz became a courier and brought some tension-relieving humor to the Watergate hearings.

The bazooka attack case illustrates the work of Special Services in the area of the activities of exiles. The people assigned to the investigation of the attack had previously been assigned to furnish security for Fidel Castro on his two prior visits and to President Dorticos of Cuba during his 1962 stay as well as to Major Guevara. The experience of these detectives demonstrates that BOSSI could carefully assign security personnel who were capable of facilitating the investigation of crimes and the related task of safeguarding the frequent targets of these crimes.

It was during Guevara's visit that we at BOSSI were first exposed to some of the dangers of unrestricted government snooping for questionable purposes. Guevara had arranged to meet a prominent American senator at a mutual friend's apartment. It was obviously to be a secret meeting, for no politician's public stature was likely to be enhanced in the 1960's by the news that he was meeting secretly with a communist leader. Federal agents, who learned of the meeting, devised an elaborate plan to photograph the senator's arrival and departure from the apartment. From across the street, the senator was photographed with his hat pulled down and his collar turned up. I am sure the senator, to this day, is unaware of the incident, but somewhere in the files of the federal government exists these photographs which, to my knowledge, have never been published.

THE MINUTEMEN CONSPIRACY

The Minutemen organization was founded in June, 1960 by Robert Bolivar De Pugh, a thirty-eight year old owner of a pharmaceutical supply house in Norborne, Missouri. The organization traces its origins to a hunting party at a Missouri lake when one of the ten men attending jokingly said, "Well, if the Russians invade us, we can come up here and fight on as a guerrilla band."(10) This quotation was the genesis of the movement and the guiding philosophy that promoted its growth.

The Minutemen subscribed to the conspiracy theory of government predicated on the betrayal of Western causes into communist hands. They considered the diplomatic war against communism as having been lost because of the actions of "bunglers and traitors within our own government." A "genuinely pro-American government here at home" was advocated, but this kind of government "could no longer be established by normal political means." The Minutemen postulated that the American public had not had an opportunity to "vote for a real American" since World War II. The "media of mass communication are effectively controlled by the enemy," and consequently, to the Minutemen no electoral reform was possible. Therefore,

> ...the objectives of the Minutemen are to abandon wasteful, useless efforts and to begin immediately to prepare for the day when Americans will once again fight in the streets for their lives and their liberty. We feel that there is overwhelming evidence to prove that this day must come ....If we do not fight them, then they will certainly fight us.

With these tenets, the organization attracted small bands of extreme rightists who saw conspiracy and communism at work everywhere in American life. The Minutemen organized themselves into "cells," i.e., individual local groups who would remain largely autonomous in order to prevent disclosure of the entire membership by one well-placed undercover agent. The Minutemen intended to function as a secret underground network while training for the hostilities to come.

The Minutemen staged para-military training exercises in the woods and stockpiled weapons and ammunition. Preparation for an unspecified, future, confrontation, however, can seldom sustain the life of any organization for long. Time and again members grew restive to attack the hated "enemy" who had the effrontery to publish newspapers and conduct political activities openly. For the Minutemen, the drift from preparation to conspiracy to direct action proved irresistible.

Ultimately they were tempted to strike the "enemy" and began to make plans to "devastate" three private recreational camps that they believed were run by communists and unions. The camps were located in New York, New Jersey, and Connecticut. To prepare to attack, the Minutemen assembled an impressive arsenal of weapons, including mortars, bazookas, machine-guns, semi-automatic rifles, home-made bombs, and more than a million rounds of ammunition.

Given the identity and objectives of the Minutemen, the Bureau of Special Services quickly determined that the group would inevitably engage in criminal activities. The Minutemen's program was explicitly subversive, and it would be a torpid intelligence unit that did not react to the group's threatened criminality. The Minutemen were under surveillance and infiltrated by BOSSI agents, and, on October 31, 1966, twenty plotters were arrested, and all of their weapons and ammunition were seized. The prisoners were charged with conspiracy to commit arson, with violation of the weapons law, and with other related charges. These arrests proved to be a body blow to the group.

From its inception in 1960, the Minutemen exhibited the classic characteristics of a subversive organization. The group was secretive, conspiratorial, extremist in its beliefs, violent in its actions, distrustful of existing government, and oriented toward a fanatical determination to resolve problems through criminal force and terrorist acts. Although its membership was not numerically large, the Minutemen constituted a threat to the peace and well-being of society, for terrorism requires few plotters to disrupt public life.

The potential dangers posed by disruptive organizations are constant, and the relative absence of such groups at any time should not lull law enforcement personnel into thinking that danger does not exist. By the time subversive groups are known to the public, perhaps as a result of a bombing or kidnapping, it is too late for an intelligence unit to effectively counter their subsequent, future acts by beginning to collect intelligence on them. By anticipating the threat of an organization like the Minutemen, Special Services met that threat with a proactive model of alertness, resourcefulness, and skill.

The thread of potential subversion that runs through America, especially involving minorities like blacks, Chicanos, and American Indians, runs through a labyrinth of turns and intersections. The infiltration of a subversive minority group may take an agent on a journey that would rival Odysseus' for its variety of adventures. The amorphous structure of the black civil rights movement has resulted in shifts of emphasis on violence and an alternation between legality and illegality. Some groups rabidly advocate violence without ever practicing it, while other organizations preach legality but break the law with alarming frequency. Some civil rights leaders like Robert F. Williams became extremely vocal pamphleteers; others, like Malcolm X matured into sophisticated and tolerant leaders.

THE BLACK LIBERATION FRONT

Before Raymond Wood was inducted into the New York City Police Department, he was a single, black man living in the South with his grandmother, with no ties to the New York City of his childhood. Both of his parents were dead, and, from all appearances, he was a promising prospect for undercover work. After he applied for police work, he was investigated, screened, interviewed, and examined, and he passed every test. He was secretly inducted into the New York City Police Department so that no unauthorized personnel ever saw a record or photograph of him that could possibly identify him with police work. He had even taken his police test in the South, thereby making the examination papers difficult to trace. Wood was to be a policeman many months before he wore a uniform and before he stepped into any official police installation.

Patrolman Wood's first assignment was to establish himself in Harlem. He found an apartment, took a series of menial jobs, and began to participate in the activities of the Bronx chapter of the Congress of Racial Equality. The chapter was then engaged in trying to integrate racially the White Castle chain of take-out food restaurants. As a result of their militancy, CORE members were engaging in breaches of law that were leading to repeated arrests. At this time the leaders of CORE in the Bronx decided to effect a citizen's arrest of then Mayor Robert F. Wagner for non-enforcement of antidiscrimination laws in the membership policies of building trades unions. When Wood and two others arrived at City Hall to arrest the mayor, they were themselves arrested, convicted, and fined.

Learning from Wood that CORE planned to arrest the Mayor allowed us at Special Services to prepare for a potentially embarrassing action. Our main problem was to avoid a jail sentence for our convicted patrolman, and we did manage to get him released after paying a fine.

Wood's arrest gave him greater credibility and acceptability with his uptown associates, and now that he was a familiar militant in the community, Wood was directed to join the Revolutionary Action Movement, a group of volatile revolutionaries who appeared ready for a public, violent action. He did not remain with the group long, for the organization did not attempt any substantial action until 1967 when sixteen members plotted to assassinate moderate civil rights leaders Roy Wilkins, Whitney Young, and others. The arrests of these sixteen in pre-dawn raids on June 21, 1967 netted an arsenal of rifles, shotguns, carbines, and other weapons and ammunition. The investigation, which briefly involved Wood, was concluded by agents of Special Services who had infiltrated the organization and had kept it under surveillance for two years before arrests were made.(12)

Patrolman Wood continued to be a popular and familiar figure in CORE, enjoying the confidence of its members. Growing discontented with CORE's lack of public action, three members eventually decided to form their own group to focus the country's attention on the plight of blacks by staging a spectacular act. The three men—Robert S. Collier, 28, Khaleel S. Sayyed, 22, and Walter Bowe, 32—formed the Black Liberation Front. Patrolman Wood was directed to move into this more promising investigative target.

The Front decided to shock the nation by blowing up a national shrine. Several monuments were considered, but the group finally decided to destroy the Statue of Liberty. Walter Bowe had lived in downtown Manhattan and used to look at the statue in the harbor and think, "if we could make that old girl blow her top we'd really put a hurt on that old bitch."(13)

Plans were made, but the group had not secured the necessary dynamite. For Wood, and the police, no overt act had been taken to further the existence of a conspiracy. Moreover, the police were interested in where and how an underground group would obtain explosives. Early in 1965, the Front contacted members of the Quebec separatist movement, and thirty sticks of dynamite were brought to New York on February 16 by Michele Duclos, a woman in the Canadian group. On that day, she and the three Front members were arrested in New York, and other arrests followed in Canada. The New York conspirators were all convicted, and all served jail sentences. Michele Duclos received probation on the condition that she would return to Canada.

Raymond Wood, the "black militant," was promoted to Detective 2nd grade and was transferred to a field assignment far removed from his former area of operations. Before he was transferred, he was required to attend the Police Academy where the presence of a Detective 2nd grade in a recruit's grey uniform caused some consternation until his undercover work was revealed. Detective Wood received the highest decoration the Police Department awards— Honorable Mention—and today he is married and is a functioning field detective.

The solutions of the Minutemen, Revolutionary Action Movement, and Black Liberation Front cases bear striking similarities. Without infiltrating these groups, Special Services could not have exposed these conspiracies until they had resulted in a violent, public act. The preventive police work effected in these cases is the hallmark of an alert intelligence unit that chooses its targets judiciously and wisely employs its personnel.

By the summer of 1975, the Watergate disclosures, the excesses attributed (and confirmed by documentation) to the FBI and the CIA, the Presidential staff's blatant misuse of federal agencies, and of the use of "enemies lists" had created such a powerful popular tide of revulsion with intelligence work that the New York *Times* on August 3rd printed the following postscript to the case of Robert S. Collier of the Black Liberation Front:

> An ultrasecretive intelligence gathering unit of the
> New York City Police Department has been de-

nounced by an Acting State Supreme Court judge for exceeding its mandate and engaging in illegal spy 'activities.'

The effect of the denunciation, and the judge's decision to dismiss the indictment of a defendant who for two years had been under surveillance, was for the first time to put the clandestine unit on notice that institutionalized "spying" violates individuals' constitutional liberties and would not be tolerated.

The function of the undercover unit, formerly called the Bureau of Special Services, is to gather intelligence on 'dissidents' who ostensibly threaten physical harm to public officials or property. In its 63-year history the unit has had a variety of names—the Radicals Bureau, the Neutrality Squad, the Public Relations Squad, BOSSI or BOSS and, most recently, the Public Security Unit of the Police Department Intelligence Division. It has had a variety of targets as well—supposed bomb throwers, German spies, labor agitators left- and right-wing 'subversives.'

Justice Peter McQuillan scored the unit's actions as he granted a defense motion to drop the state's two-year-old indictment against Robert Steele Collier, who in 1973 was charged with conspiring to possess explosives and illegal possession of a gun. Ten years ago Mr. Collier was convicted of conspiring to blow up the Statue of Liberty and other national monuments. In May 1971 he was acquitted in the 'Panther 13' trial on charges of conspiring to blow up police stations and other public buildings. A few days after the acquittal, a BOSS agent was 'planted' in the Lower East Side community where Mr. Collier lived. The agent kept up surveillance for two years, during which he searched apartments, duplicated keys, and occasionally confiscated photos and writing samples.

Justice McQuillan said there was no probable cause at that time to suspect criminal activity to justify the BOSS infiltration and that the evidence that led to the 1973 indictment evolved a full year and a half after the surveillance began. His decision, he said, was intended not to thwart legitimate undercover police work necessitated by evidence of criminal activity but to curb an 'open-ended free-wheeling people-watching mission.'(14)

Justice McQuillan's decision, is instructive for the guidance it furnishes on the use of undercover operators:

It rests with courts to reconcile the legitimate intelligence needs of law enforcement with constitutional rights...

The law enforcement establishment exists to prevent criminal conduct and to arrest offenders. Stealth is often a necessary strategy for certain situations. Thus, the deceptive use of undercover operatives to infiltrate a very limited group is permissible when the police believe or suspect that criminal conduct is taking place or may be anticipated. *Lewis v. United States,* 385 U.S. 206; *Hoffa v. United States,* 385 U.S. 293; *Osborn v. United States,* 385 U.S. 323, 331-2.

The gathering of evidence against certain offenders is frequently a difficult task. 'Thus in drug-related offenses law enforcement personnel have turned to one of the only practicable means of detection: the infiltration of drug rings and a limited participation in their unlawful present practices. Such infiltration is a recognized and permissible means of investigation... *United States v. Russell,* 411 U.S. 423, 432.

The danger from bombings and arsons by depraved cretins posing as revolutionaries necessitates firm measures by government. Undercover operatives often perform difficult and dangerous assignments to assure domestic tranquility. While we can never expect a state of perfect order and security, the goal of an open society is to defend itself against the tyranny of the lawless in a manner that comports with constitutional limitations . . .

An infiltrator may be planted in a group only when the police have articulable reasons to believe or suspect that criminal activity is afoot, and the operation should continue only until sufficient evidence is obtained to warrant an arrest. (See the June, 1975 Rockefeller Commission Report: 'Any intrusive investigation of an American citizen by the government must have a sufficient basis to warrant the invasion caused by the particular investigative practices which are utilized . . .The scope of any resulting intrusion on personal privacy must not exceed the degree reasonably believed necessary; . . .these conditions must be met . . .to the satisfaction of . . .a court.')

When an undercover operative represents himself as 'game for anything' this kind of pose tends to generate a dangerous aggressiveness by the operative. And the risk of provocation is always inherent in any infiltration operation. The potential for abuse is enormous. (See Zimroth, *op. cit.:* 'The obvious danger in police methods like these is that the police are sometimes promoting the very activities they say they are trying to prevent. An undercover agent cannot be effective unless he is accepted, and he will not be accepted unless he participates in the activities of the group. But sometimes the fear of being discovered will lead agents or informants to be more vocal and more militant than the people they are investigating'(p. 62-3).Undercover operations . . .sometimes bring with them threats to civil liberties—entrapment, provocation, weakening of people's willingness to join controversial organizations. But the existence of these possibilities does not inexorably lead to a blanket condemnation of undercover agents in all circumstances'(p. 91.) . . .

Police infiltration must be condemned when the exercise of such power is not bounded by precise and clear standards. Infiltration should occur under procedural safeguards designed to obviate the danger of unreasonable impairment of privacy. Insistence for such safeguards is "but a special instance of the larger principle that freedoms of expression must be ringed about with adequate bulwarks. *Bantam Books, Inc. v. Sullivan,* 372 U.S. 58, 66.

Professionals in investigative work had brought public and judicial distrust of their activities down upon themselves, and it appears that public confidence in intelligence work can be restored in the future only when that public needs information to maintain its own safety. Perhaps that need will be expressed more quickly than we think as Presidential assassinations are attempted, kidnappings occur, and international terrorism increases.

THE PROGRESSIVE LABOR MOVEMENT

On January 27, 1966 in the Manhattan Criminal Court building, William Epton of the Progressive Labor Movement was convicted of anarchy while the killers of Malcolm X were standing trial. The dramatic stories that were unfolding in separate court rooms were years in the making.

The Progressive Labor Movement(15) is a Peking-oriented communist organization, with a small membership of perhaps fifty to a hundred casual and devoted adherents. The goal of the Movement is to replace democratic government in America with a new communist state. To achieve its goal, members engage in activities calculated to foment discord, erode public confidence in police, and weaken government. The leaders of the Movement are at least second generation communists. If one's parents were not members of the Party, a member was unable to reach the councils of leadership in the Movement. Since conspiracy is planned by the highest echelon of a group, an effort by a new member or an undercover agent to infiltrate the leadership of the Movement was generally impossible.

The Progressive Labor Movement, first organized in early 1962, busily exploited the chaos furnished by the Harlem riots of 1964. On July 16th, James Powell, a black youngster, was shot by Police Lieutenant Thomas Gilligan who had intervened in the assault of a janitor. Acting under the name of the Harlem Defense Council, a typical front group created for the convenience of the moment, the PLM attempted to launch a march on a Harlem police station house, printed incendiary leaflets, and persistently harangued people with the need to attack police. Bill Epton, a PLM member, was particularly vocal in calling for the death of police. Later, a grand jury investigating the role of the PLM in maintaining the momentum of the riots indicted several members for contempt when they refused to answer questions relating to the disorders. The members were jailed, and an injunction barring demonstrations by the Progressive Labor Movement was sought and granted. Bill Epton was indicted for anarchy in connection with his call for people to kill police and judges on July 18th and was convicted. His one year sentence was appealed. It is interesting that the Harlem riots in 1964 started seven hours after Epton had made a street corner speech.

The reaction in Harlem to the shooting of James Powell was a typically skillful exploitation by the PLM of public resentment of a police shooting that was to blacks a highly questionable act.

A decade later public resentment with the police did not need the reenforcement of a subversive organization. When a Puerto Rican prisoner hanged himself in a police precinct cell, his friends charged police with brutality and murder. The Police Department merely issued an impersonal statement concerning its "continuing investigation of the death," hoping as it did ten years ago, that such a statement would end the matter. Subsequently, a phone call was made to call the police to a booby-trapped building. A young police officer, ironically Hispanic, responded to the call and lost an eye when the door of the building blew up in his face. Within ten years, the public's resentment with police had changed its mode of expression from street rioting to individual acts of terrorism. The public arena had, in this case, been totally dominated by the friends and relatives of the deceased and their charges of police murder. The Police Department had lost contact with the people in that arena and had paid the price—a wounded police officer—for its lack of understanding.

In retrospect, the Harlem riots were not caused by extremist elements; they, like Puerto Rican discontent later, were caused by people's dissatisfaction with unemployment, education, housing, and their general state of being. Extremist groups like the PLM did, however, exploit these discontents, as they did in Newark in 1967, (16).

As a result of quick identification and arrest of Progressive Labor Movement members, the group eventually ceased to be active.(17) Every significant development in the investigation of the PLM was initiated by Special Services which had, in addition to the continuous overt investigation of the group, infiltrated the organization with Abe Hart, a policeman who had been recruited in Pittsburgh. Hart was able to circumvent the Movement's normal caution and security policies, because he was obviously not a New Yorker and because he was black.

THE ASSASSINATION OF MALCOLM X

The assassination, by his former comrades, of Malcolm X Little, on February 21, 1965, in the Audubon Ballroom in Harlem, had been foreseen by Special Services at least two weeks before the killing occurred. That an assassination would be attempted was predicated on bits of information flowing into BOSSI that indicated that Malcolm's disagreements with the Nation of Islam were potentially, very dangerous. Malcolm was offered police protection on at least three occasions, before witnesses, two weeks before his death. These offers, reported in the press, did much to weaken the later contentions of Malcolm's followers that the police were indifferent to his plight. At BOSSI we did realize that a police bodyguard would cramp Malcolm's free moving style in crowds and that he would probably refuse it.

Malcolm X Little was born on May 19, 1925 and had an eighth grade education. He was converted to the Nation of Islam while serving a ten-year prison term for robbery in Massachusetts. Upon his release in 1952 after serving six years, he became a leader in the Nation of Islam.

The Nation of Islam, or Black Muslims, had been founded in Detroit in 1930 by W.D. Fard, an itinerant Eurasian peddler who convinced many blacks that they were the chosen people. He attracted to the Nation of Islam many members of the Marcus Garvey movement of black nationalism, which had collapsed in the late 1920's. Fard wedded black supremacy to his concepts of the Mohammedan religion and selected and trained a staff of ministers. His chief minister became Elijah Poole, who used the name, Elijah Muhammad. Fard disappeared mysteriously in 1934, and Poole became the leader of the Black Muslims, the headquarters of which was moved to Chicago. Elijah Muhammad died in 1975, and was succeeded by his son, Wallace Muhammad, who quickly moved to liberalize the Black Muslims.

Having joined the Nation of Islam, Malcolm, back in New York City, quickly found room for the expression of his many talents. He was a brilliant speaker, an effective organizer, a tireless recruiter, and a charismatic leader. As head of the New York Mosque, Malcolm X became a problem to Elijah Muhammad, who sought not only to retain his national leadership but also to transfer power to his sons and son-in-law. Malcolm was an obstacle to these plans, and when he referred to President Kennedy's assassination as "the chickens coming home to roost," Elijah Muhammad suspended, and subsequently expelled, Malcolm from the Nation of Islam.

With Malcolm's expulsion, the Nation of Islam was wracked with dissension that reached Muhammad's own family. Two of his sons joined Malcolm for a time. Malcolm attacked Muhammad personally, when he accused the older man of fathering several illegitimate babies with Black Muslim secretaries. That attack was bound to have serious consequences, as Malcolm himself predicted.

After Malcolm's expulsion from the Nation of Islam, he founded the Organization of Afro-American Unity which attracted many members of the Black Muslims. The OAAU collapsed after Malcolm's death. Leon Ameer, one of the presumed heirs to Malcolm, was found dead in a hotel room in Boston only a few weeks after Malcolm's assassination. Mae Collins, Malcolm's sister, assumed leadership of the OAAU, but the vitality was drained from the organization after the death of its leader and founder.

The work of Special Services helped to solve the murder of Malcolm X. A newspaper account of the assassination reported:

> Several undercover plainclothes policemen were in the uptown meeting hall at the time Malcolm X was shot dead there on Sunday.
>
> According to a high police official, several members of its outstanding unit the highly secretive Bureau of Special Services (BOSS), were in the Audubon Ballroom at Broadway and 166th

Street, when bullets cut down Malcolm X as he started to address a group of 400 persons, ostensibly all devoted to him.(18)

Three men were arrested and convicted of Malcolm X's murder. One of them, Norman 3 X Butler, was described as a Black Muslim enforcer who, when Malcolm was assassinated, was free on bail in the shooting of another Black Muslim defector a month earlier. Another footnote to the assassination of Malcolm X was the identity of one of Malcolm's closest associates, who received a bullet hole in his jacket during the shooting and who was photographed by *Life* magazine, giving him mouth-to-mouth resuscitation. The man was a BOSSI agent.

The Nation of Islam(19) is estimated to have in the United States a hundred thousand members, of which a third probably represents the group's true strength. It is a separatist group that, notwithstanding its small size, was, until 1975 when Wallace Muhammad assumed leadership, a state within the state, profoundly alienated, non-cooperative, and basically hostile to the rest of society. The strength of the Nation of Islam was inversely related to that of the civil rights movement; as one gained strength, the other lost strength.

The personal standards imposed by the Nation of Islam on its members are strict and are often intended as rehabilitative. Members may not smoke, drink alcohol, or engage in any immoral behavior. The group is disciplined and puritanical. Its clashes with authority have been spontaneous reactions to real or imagined intrusions. Although the group had not embarked on a policy of violence, its goals imply potential conflict as C. Eric Lincoln has noted:

> The expectation of an eventual racial clash is widespread among observers who know the movement first hand . . . The ultimate appeal of the Movement, therefore, is the chance to become

identified with a power strong enough to overcome the combination of the white man—and perhaps even to subordinate him in turn.(20)

The racism, separatism, and violence preached and occasionally practiced by the Black Muslims may be of possible future concern, although Wallace Muhammad's leadership seems to be turning the group from racial separatism. Ironically, the strength and discipline of the older organization has been responsible for showing corrections people how to rehabilitate convicts. Many older members of the Nation of Islam, doing much of their poselytizing in jail, have succeeded in teaching fellow convicts how to return successfully to society.

The International Association of Chiefs of Police conducted two surveys of the administration of police departments in two cities. The first study made the following comments on intelligence units:

> The purpose of an Intelligence Section is to keep the Commissioner informed. . . .on the structure, membership and plans of secret organizations engaged in subversive activities.
>
> The function of information-gathering will include the development of confidential informants . . .and a close liaison with agents in other Federal, State and local agencies.(21)

A similar survey undertaken two years later made the following observations on the intelligence function:

> The mission of the proposed Inspectional Services Bureau is to obtain and provide the police commissioner with significant information about the environment in which the New York City Police Department operates and about response of the department to its environment. . . .

Modern society is faced with the problems of controlling a substantial number of people who knowingly or unknowingly are contributing to the destruction of society....The competent police administrator in every large urban community in the United States is obligated to keep himself informed about the identity and activities of these police hazards. It is the mission of the intelligence function of the department to identify such persons and to be informed about their activities. . ...As the tensions of modern society increase, the problems involved in maintaining peace and order are also increasing. Since the police are charged with the responsibility for preserving domestic tranquility and maintaining the public peace, it is important that the department be knowledgeable about those who would create disorder.(22)

The two reports clearly illustrate a growing awareness of the danger that civil disorder creates for society. The riots that became an urban phenomenon in the 1960's were not caused by subversives. It is, however, becoming increasingly obvious that dissident criminal elements do play a role in sustaining and exacerbating urban tensions. Riot reports repeatedly refer to groups spreading rumors, haranguing crowds, distributing incendiary pamphlets and in every way seeking to create disorder. The violence that reached a peak in Detroit in the summer of 1967 is a continuing problem for police intelligence, because it is produced by disciplined groups who are more militantly involved with causes than the dissidents of the 1960's.

The black writer, Louis Lomax, writing about the Newark riot of July, 1967, made the following observations in a brilliant series of articles:

Newark, New Jersey has become the hub of Black Power and revolutionary activity in America, particularly along the East Coast and the Midwest.

Black Power revolutionaries from Detroit, were in Newark when that city erupted in July. They departed for their home town to aid in carrying out an even greater holocaust.

Revolutionaries from Newark were in Peekskill, New York, and New Haven, Conn., as "observers" when those cities broke with riots. The same is true for Syracuse, New York.

Not only were Newark's black revolutionaries in Plainfield, New Jersey, when that city erupted but there was a direct connection between the arms stolen in Plainfield and the cache of machine guns and carbines now resting in a Newark slum basement.

Black power militant, H. Rap Brown made a clandestine visit to Newark shortly before he was arrested on a federal gun charge in New York. Much soberer, more determined and less flamboyant black revolutionaries in Newark lectured Brown for carrying the carbine that led to his all but ludicrous arrest three nights later.

Newark's black revolutionaries are the most sought after "consultants" in the nation. Just last week a caravan of 25 black revolutionaries from Washington, D.C., motored to Newark's Black Power headquarters along South Sixth Street for "advice and assistance."

Needless to report, Newark's black revolutionaries played a significant role in the burning and looting and shooting that scarred their own town. They are, of course, actively planning another rebellion.(23)

In his five articles, Mr Lomax validates his observations with personal interviews, eyewitness reports, and first hand investigative reporting.

The neutralization of subversive elements would unquestionably result in greatly reducing the destruction and violence that attend urban riots. In New York City, the experience in controlling actual and incipient riots has been successful, primarily because police administrators had the information upon which to act resolutely. The exposure and prosecution of conspirators have discouraged others from urban rioting and violence. Due in part to the effective and extensive activities of BOSSI, the price of subversion in New York City is higher than most plotters are willing to pay.

Although undercover agents like Raymond Wood and Abe Hart conducted investigative operations in the field, they, and BOSSI, never became involved—and should not have become involved in the operations—arrests, roundups, questioning—of the Police Department. Except for the mistaken arrest of Wood, the intelligence function (BOSSI) and the operational function (NYCPD) were kept apart. Others have urged this separation:

> The primary purpose of our Intelligence Unit is to gather, record, evaluate and exchange information on individuals, organizations and conditions found in San Francisco.(24)

> The Central Intelligence Agency should have nothing to do with policy. It should try to get at the hard facts on which others must determine policy.(25)

> Without proper intelligence and its rapid evaluation, police operations in this area will usually be ineffective.(26)

Any intelligence agency will be strongly pressured and tempted to engage in the follow-up operations that its acquisition of intelligence indicates. This temptation must be resisted. An intelligence agency that has been given operational responsibilities generally drifts away from intelligence gathering, justifies favorite projects, and begins to eliminate from consideration that data which does not conform to operational requirements. When operations are left to other groups (usually a police department), the intelligence unit is able to forward all information objectively, and consequently the needs of the operating agency will serve to doublecheck the methods of the intelligence agency.

Although intelligence gathering and operations have traditionally been kept separate in this country, in a dictatorship they are usually merged into a repressive and terrifying force. In one of the more mysterious and unresolved cases in which BOSSI was involved, one can, from the known details of the case, surmise what the underlying power of a secret state intelligence unit may be.

THE DISAPPEARANCE OF JESUS DE GALINDEZ

Rafael Trujillo had a well-earned reputation for extending the reach of his power beyond the borders of the Dominican Republic. His predilection for vengeance led to New York City on March 12, 1956.

After fighting in the Spanish Civil War, Jesus de Galindez was exiled from his country and fled to the Dominican Republic where he held a number of teaching and governmental advisory posts from 1940 to 1946 and where he, born a Basque, championed that province's independence from Spain. His life in the Dominican Republic, under another dictator like Franco, left him a bitter foe of Trujillo's regime. When he came to the United States in 1946, he expressed his opposition in speeches, lectures, and his writings. He became the representative of the Basque Government in Exile and continued his studies toward a doctorate at Columbia University. His thesis, *The Era of Trujillo*, was a devastating and scholarly denunciation of the dictator's regime.

de Galindez knew he was in danger. Some of his former

associates had disappeared and were presumably dead. He frequently expressed his fears and had, at least once, experienced an encounter with a man, probably Trujillo's agent, who tried to kill him. At the age of forty-two, single, tall, slim, and serious, Jesus de Galindez was driven home from a class he was teaching at Columbia. On a late winter evening, he got out of the car and was never seen again.

It became evident that Trujillo had decreed a harsh fate for de Galindez. Months later, Gerry Murphy, an American pilot, recognized a photograph of de Galindez as a passenger he had flown to the Dominican Republic, because he was terminally ill with cancer and wanted to visit his mother. Murphy had falsified airport records in Amityville, Long Island, to escape detection by immigration authorities.

The photo recognition was to cost Murphy his life, He quickly told his fiance of the identification and the possible danger he might encounter. After he put his car and home furnishings up for sale, he disappeared. Later, the Trujillo government announced that Murphy disappeared in the shark-infested waters off Cuidad Trujillo, now part of Santo Domingo. His killer, Octavio de la Maza, claimed that he was spurning Murphy's homosexual advances, that they had fought, and that Murphy fell over a cliff into the sea. To us at BOSSI, the use of homosexuality in the announcement indicated Trujillo's involvement, for his favorite sobriquets were "communist" and "homosexual"; Trujillo knew how to pander to American paranoia and prejudice.

We were told that de la Maza was in jail, but it was not until Murphy's congressman, Charles O. Porter, insisted that the State Department investigate the case that further developments occurred. The inquiries of American authorities resulted in the production of de la Maza's corpse. According to the Trujillo regime, de la Maza, remorseful about his killing, had hanged himself with mosquito netting in his cell. After inspecting the cell, investigators were doubtful that a man could hang himself in it.

de Galindez's fate has never been definitely established. A

world wanderer, writer, and general man of mystery, he played many roles that have never been fully explored. Trujillo's hiring of former employees of the federal government; his use of diplomats for criminal acts; his merciless pursuit of his foes; de Galindez's own mysterious and unreported activities; and the possible involvement of BOSSI personnel and people identified with Watergate will eventually reveal the outlines of a fascinating case in which intelligence gathering and police operations were used with unprecedented power and illegality.

The Bureau of Special Services has consistently avoided operational functions; the unit does not even arrest conspirators after all evidence on them has been gathered by the Bureau. Actual arrests are usually made by field units of the New York City Police Department. Every demonstration, dispute, or disorder is policed by other units of the Police Department. The one major exception, when BOSSI is functioning operationally, occurs in providing escorts; in these cases, the knowledge and experience of Special Services personnel require their operational involvement.

The small number of employees in BOSSI also serves to keep the unit's attention firmly focused on intelligence gathering, not operations. The voluminous amount of work generated by a large city like New York tends to keep BOSSI from fulfilling all non-essential operations. Finally, the persistent, growing need of the New York City Police Department for accurate information serves to keep Special Services busy supplying data to the Department which then must act on its own to contain, control, and cope with the disruptions and subversion indicated in the gathered intelligence.

In the rhetoric of the 1960's, we were continually reminded that "disruptions" occurred, but "subversion," with its implications of wartime espionage and of the McCarthy inquiries into communism, fell into disuse. Euphemisms abounded. It became easier to discuss "destabilizing" a government than "subverting" it. The "interdiction of enemy forces" seems a nobler pursuit than the destruction of those who oppose others. It is certainly more convenient and fashionable to refer to "offing the pigs" than to refer to killing men and women who are police. The psychological import of jargon lies in its casting a protective, concealing mantle over fact. That people and groups continue to plan and execute public murder for political and social purposes should remind the public that subversion, nevertheless, continues to exist and that the best defense against it is intelligence gathered effectively and legally.

The problem in law and in law enforcement is to determine the balance between the protection of society and the preservation of individual rights. Every intelligence operation constitutes an intrusion on privacy, and consequently intelligence agencies must be legally supervised. However, they must also be permitted to be effective.

Some intelligence operations are clearly illegal. When the FBI in the 1960's infiltrated extremist groups to obtain information to harass and intimidate members, the agency was beginning to abuse its power to violate individual rights. That the FBI continued to abuse its power was made more explicit in 1975 with disclosures prompted by newspaper reporters' inquiries under the Freedom of Information Act—a law that should inhibit illicit operations. The inquiries revealed that the FBI had sent to Jewish communists anonymous missives describing Russia's anti-semitism, had written anonymously to Ku Klux Klan members to tell them that their identity was known, had harassed the American Nazi Party from its Chicago headquarters, had sent a letter suggesting suicide to Martin Luther King Jr., and had issued false news releases announcing the fall of Klan leaders. Clearly the FBI had failed to ask itself whether what it was doing was legal . . .or right.

In the early 1960's, BOSSI was tempted, like the FBI, to harass the Black Muslims. Under Muhammad and Malcolm, the Black Muslims looked like a growing threat to urban peace. The group seemed to be a state within a state. Their discipline, militancy, and profound alienation (characterized by their song, "A White Man's Heaven is a Black Man's Hell") seemed to pose real danger and potential violence. To some people in BOSSI, the key to defusing the organization seemed to lie in separating Muhammad and Malcolm. A plan was proposed to send Muhammad a letter containing some facts about Malcolm that would cast him as a potential usurper and threat to Muhammad's leadership. The proposal was considered, discussed, and finally rejected. Adopting the plan would have eroded BOSSI's moral base and would have turned it into the police terror group that its critics claimed it had become.

The effectiveness of any single agency will rest on the existence of a coordinated criminal justice system that confronts the challenge posed by any problem of criminality and devises a solution for that problem. A police department and its units must be seen as a part of a national criminal justice system of cooperative, integrated, and coordinated parts that function in concert. The delicate orchestration of all parts of the criminal justice system has proved elusive. Each group within the system, whether it is the FBI, the CIA, or a local police department, has played its own music, and the result has been a cacophony of failures instead of the harmony of orchestrated successes.

CHAPTER V.

Security for Dignitaries

The responsibility for the safety of all residents of and visitors to New York City rests with the Police Department. Public Law 357 of the Eightieth Congress requires that the appropriate American authorities (the New York City Police Department) provide police protection to the United Nations and to the people working there. Under international protocol and comity, the responsibility for safeguarding representatives of foreign countries falls upon the host nation. Even the President of the United States becomes the responsibility of the Police Department when he visits New York City, despite the primary responsibility of the United States Secret Service for his security.

The enormous increase in international political activities, especially evidenced by the frequent visits of heads of state, have greatly magnified the importance of security assignments. After World War II, only occasional and highly publicized visits, required the casual attention of the police. Today, the annual visits of heads of state and other dignitaries number in the hundred, and their safety is essential because of the international ramifications of any violent attack upon them.

The New York City Police Department charges the Bureau of Special Services with the specific responsibility of coordinating, planning, and preparing all security requirements connected with the visits of dignitaries. Special Services' security function grew naturally from its liaisons with other agencies and its investigation of subversive activities.

Three functions—liaison, investigation, and security—are all part of the administration of Special Services, and these functions complement each other while contributing to the success of the overall mission.

George Bernard Shaw said that "assassination is the extreme form of censorship." Most dictionaries define "assassinate" as "murder by sudden or secret attack" and "assassin" as a "murderer, especially one that kills either for hire or from fanatical motives." Assassination has been political reality since the day people allowed one man to make decisions for them and the disaffected sought to contravene the decision-maker by resorting to the veto of personal violence. Throughout history, references are made to successful or attempted assassinations which altered the course of human events by the single dramatic act of violently ending one man's life. Greek drama contains references to the assassination of Agammemnon, the murder of King Laius by his son, Oedipus, and the killing of King Eurytus by an enraged Hercules. People have killed their leaders in every civilization, and assassination continues to be a drastic means of social change today. Regicide was no stranger in the United States on November 22, 1963.

The visit of twenty-six heads of state to the fifteenth General Assembly of the United Nations in New York City in September, 1960, represented an unprecedented challenge to the New York City Police Department. It also gave Special Services an opportunity to cope with new experiences in the field of security. The visit made the Police Department more aware of the intricacies of security and focused attention on the need for more sophisticated approaches to the problem of safeguarding dignitaries. At BOSSI, we had never encountered the large number of logistical problems of coordinating security measures. It seemed as if demonstrators from twenty-six countries were on the streets where the political left of each country picketed the political right. In addition, hundreds of exiles were determined to harass the hated leaders who had driven them from their former homes.

The anti-Castro Cubans, the anti-Khrushchev Hungarians, the opponents of Nasser, Sukarno, Tito, *et. al.* represented serious potential threats to the security of the visitors who nevertheless arrived, functioned, and departed without incident.

The visit of Pope Paul VI on October 4, 1965 (1) represented another unique security experience for Special Services. The Pope did not have a group of organized opponents as the national leaders at the UN had had. The Pope's status as a religious leader and the inevitable attraction of religion to psychotics made him a particularly vulnerable target for a deranged person. Martin Luther King Jr. became the target of an unsuccessful knife attack by a psychotic in Harlem just before his assassination in Memphis. It is common knowledge among law enforcement officers that the mentally ill frequently suffer religious hallucinations resulting from deep social and political grievances. Symbolic leaders like the Pope or Martin Luther King Jr. become the targets of the deranged who come to feel that their grievances can be ended by killing a religious leader.

The Pope's visit required the tireless and devoted attention of BOSSI security forces who never relaxed during the constant television coverage of the Pope's itinerary. Such visits provide Special Services personnel with invaluable knowledge of the difficult area of personal security, and this experience has been welded to the various ethnic, cultural, and national backgrounds of the people in BOSSI who represent many of the world's countries and who speak most of the world's major languages.

Of the thirty-five men who have been Presidents of the United States, four have been assassinated. Abraham Lincoln was shot by an ardent secessionist in 1865; James Garfield was killed by a disgruntled office-seeker in 1881; an American anarchist assassinated William McKinley in 1901(2); and John F. Kennedy was killed by a leftist mystic in 1963. The thought of assassination is seldom far from the minds of statesmen. President Kennedy said, "If someone is going to kill me, they are going to kill me."(3) As if in echo, Adolf Hitler had said in 1941, " . . .I can be eliminated at any moment by a criminal or a lunatic."(4) At least three different, carefully planned, and professionally executed attempts were made upon Charles de Gaulle's life. During the last twenty years, four Latin American leaders have been assassinated: Jose Remon of Panama in 1956, Anastasio Somoza of Nicaragua in 1956, Carlos Castillo Armas of Guatemala in 1958, and Rafael Trujillo of the Dominican Republic in 1961. Four heads of emerging African states have fallen: Patrice Lumumba of the Congo in 1961, Sylvanus Olympio of Togo in 1965, Sir Abubakar Tafewa Balewa of Nigeria and his successor, Major General Johnson T.U. Aguiji-Ironsi both in 1966. In the Arab states, King Abdullah Ibn Hussein of Jordan in 1951, King Faisal in 1957 and Premier Abdul Karim Kassem, in 1963 both of Iraq, and King Faisal of Saudi Arabia all died at the hands of assassins. In the Orient, Ghandi of India in 1948, S.W.R.D. Bandaranaike of Nepal in 1959, and Ngo Dinh Diem of South Vietnam in 1964 all met sudden death. The Union of South Africa lost Premier Hendrik Frensch Verwoerd to an assassin's knife in 1966.

Of these political assassinations, only India, Nepal, and the United States had free societies at the time of the deaths of their leaders. The other twelve countries were governed with varying degrees of repression, including Nazi Germany where the July 1944 plot to kill Hitler almost succeeded.

Freedom necessarily increases the security risk of national leaders. The Warren Commission concluded that security was made more difficult and, inferentially, the police were less likely to prevent a successful attack, in a free society. The Commission believed that the development of a garrison state would, at least, make the safety of American Presidents an easier matter. Probably the many grievances inevitably created by an oppressive regime automatically produces conspirators who are likely to use murder as a means of political change. Although providing security for leaders in a democracy is difficult without constraints, it is less likely that a truly free society will produce people whose only political recourse is assassination.

Attempts to kill a leader, or assassinations, by definition and experience, fell into two categories at BOSSI:

> 1. The motivated. Persons or groups with a real or imagined grievance who have conspired to kill the head of state by way of achieving their ends. The July plot against Hitler, the attempts against DeGaulle and the attempt against President Truman by Puerto Rican Nationalists on November 1, 1950 are classic examples of this type. These plotters had a definite aim and a specific policy in mind, notwithstanding the merit of their position.
> 2. The demented. Those who irrationally focus their animus on a prominent person and see their salvation in terms of the elimination of this statesman.(5)

Since the anticipated sources of an attack are more or less clearly identified by the two categories above, it follows that security measures (watching crowds for protesters, checking threats from the mentally deranged) must be tailored to these categories, and the security measures taken must anticipate the likely nature of an attack and stop it. A prime aid in detecting a motivated assassin is that he or she acts logically, and motives can usually be deduced and anticipated.

The threat to an American President arises generally from any group of the permanently disaffected. Racist groups see the elimination of the President as the first step toward a return to the "white American way of life;" extreme rightists fear that a President is soft on communism; and leftists see terror and the overthrow of the President and the government as the key to their victory. Added to these groups are Puerto Rican Nationalists who may view the killing of the President as the first essential step toward independence for their island, Black Nationalist groups who promote assassination as a potential expression of their anger and frustration, and the psychotic who, because of an act, or an imagined act, of a President, develop a consuming, driving passion to eliminate the man who has become a target to be destroyed.

A set of regulations issued by the Warren Commission to the FBI on December 26, 1963, describes those who threaten the President as:

> Subversives, ultrarightists, racists and fascists (a) possessing emotional instability or irrational behavior, (b) who have made threats of bodily harm against officials or employees of Federal, state or local government or officials of a foreign government, (c) who express or have expressed strong or violent anti-U.S. sentiments and who have been involved in bombing or bomb-making or whose past conduct indicates tendencies toward violence, and (d) whose prior acts or statements depict propensity for violence and hatred against organized government.(6)

This statement supplemented the regulation that the FBI should forward to the United States Secret Service all information that indicated a possible attempt against the person or safety of the President. A notable violation of the first regulation was the FBI's destruction of a Lee Harvey Oswald letter days after the assassination of John F. Kennedy.

The security of other dignitaries poses problems that are different only in degree, not in kind, from the problems of Presidential security. Exile groups from many nations have found a haven in the United States, but their antipathy for their former governments or leaders is sharply aroused when a representative of that government arrives for a visit. Although the arrival of any member of the Castro government poses serious security problems, a personal visit by Fidel Castro would magnify these difficulties significantly.

New York City has always been a temporary home for expatriates from oppressed countries. Exiles today differ from earlier expatriates only to the degree that the focus of oppression shifts with history. Fifteen years ago the city hosted exiles fleeing the tyrannies of Batista and Trujillo; still earlier, European despotism brought waves of exiles to Ellis Island. Later, the city housed Hungarian and Yugoslav exiles whose opposition to communism required police protection of the Yugoslav consulate and mission at all times. The Middle East crisis of June, 1967 resulted in round-the-clock police guard of the missions of all participants in that war. Recently, exiled revolutionaries of countries like Libya, Cuba, and Iraq require surveillance in that they can be potential terrorists capable of skyjackings and kidnappings. The degree of sensitivity of any foreign dignitary's visit is generally related to the amount of oppression in his country and the disaffection among exiles, and, as police noted during Yassir Arafat's visit to the UN, even among the general American population.

Security for visiting dignitaries, as well as for the President, is arranged through the Bureau of Special Services. The unit serves as a nucleus for the New York City Police Department's planning and operations concerning security matters. However, the Secret Service does have primary responsibility for the President's personal safety, and the Department of State assigns a security force to visiting heads of state. These forces, however, have to be substantially supplemented by local agencies because of manpower limitations and, in the case of New York City, the complexity and size of locale. Supplementary personnel are especially needed by the Department of State for heads of state, because the Department has only a limited number of people to assign to security and because its primary interest is in international diplomacy.

From the moment that an announcement is made to the New York City Police Department that a President or a foreign dignitary will visit the city, the following procedures are followed.

The Secret Service, or the personal security force for a dignitary, sends to the city an advance team which proposes an itinerary. A conference is held at which all relevant units of the Police Department are represented. Every detail of the itinerary is discussed. Routes and alternate routes are selected. Difficulties likely to be encountered at any given stop are weighed and analyzed. Identification devices (badges, cards) to be used to enter or leave restricted areas are selected and disseminated. Every agency of government that might be affected by the visit is invited to attend the conference, including airport authorities or official security personnel from any place, like a museum or power plant, that is on the itinerary.

The necessary orders are printed and disseminated on the basis of all preliminary meetings and conferences. Confidential matters are closely guarded. Orders and information must be quickly disseminated to those people who are charged with the responsibility of the visit.

A mock visit or dry run-through at every location to be visited is then planned. This exercise should reveal any vulnerable locations, possible detours, or unforeseen road obstacles, and should give security personnel complete familiarity with physical layouts. The run-through is also a valuable supplement to security planning in that it reveals needs and hazards that cannot be envisioned from headquarters and permits the most logical and useful assignment of personnel. Plans can also be made to search and secure various sites several hours prior to the arrival of the official party. The pre-arrival security operation involves a search of areas, a check of utilities, facilities, and the entire physical layout, and the assignment of someone to guard an area once it has been secured.

When the late General Rafael Trujillo of the Dominican Republic came to New York, he had a complete dental unit installed in his quarters for convenient use by his family and himself. All the equipment was made in the United States, and all of the wiring and installation had been done by Dominicans. On the day that the installation was completed,

Trujillo proudly approached the chair to demonstrate the equipment. His dentist, an American, intervened and turned on the equipment himself. The wires had not been properly grounded, and the unfortunate dentist was knocked to the ground by a jolt of electricity. Although the accident undoubtedly resulted from careless oversight, rather than any deliberate attempt to harm, it would have been diplomatically embarrassing if the dictator had been personally injured.

After a run-through of the itinerary, the automobiles or other conveyances to be used by the official party must be secured, and plans for the continuous security of these vehicles must be formulated. Plans must also be made for the interception of packages as well as for the fluoroscoping of any suspicious parcels. The Bomb Squad is alerted to examine packages and to search buildings, following any anonymous bomb threats. The Bomb Squad can completely search a plane in which a bomb may be planted, and recently the Squad has been using dogs that are trained to sniff out explosives.

Employees like waiters, hotel maids, and elevator operators likely to come into contact with the official party are given a security check. In the case of Presidential security, security checks involve the use of Secret Service and BOSSI files which have been compiled and evaluated over the years but which recently have been reduced due to court decisions. Because it is impossible to anticipate everyone who will come into contact with an official party, occasionally a potential threat may be discovered during an official function; on such an occasion, intelligence agents will subtly deflect the employee or other potentially dangerous person from the area.

Every location affected, including, of course, the temporary residence of the visiting party, must be surveyed for handling demonstrations. Sites must be selected for picketing and counterpicketing. These sites must not, by their nature, blunt the effectiveness of the demonstration; if they do, their selection constitutes an infringement of constitutional rights. At these demonstration sites, the safety of the visiting dignitary must be assured. Police must consider the possible side-effects of a demonstration. Probable violence, disorder, large groups of people, clashes between opposing factions as well as possible attempts against a visiting dignitary's life must be weighed, and plans to handle such an eventuality must be carefully prepared.

The routes to be used by the visitors are traveled and examined by local and federal security forces twenty-four hours and, later, four hours prior to their actual use by visitors. If any changes in the routes are required, they are made. Commanders are assigned sectors along the route, especially near overpasses, roofs, large gatherings of people, or any vulnerable location. In a large crowd, the sector commander must be cognizant of such dangers as excessive congestion, panic, or disorderly demonstrations. Using detectives to supplement uniformed coverage is another indispensable condition of security. Some basic but important crowd-control techniques should be used by uniformed personnel. They must, for example, always face the spectators, and they should generally be placed between the official party and the crowd of onlookers. Barriers should be used to supplement manpower in crowded situations. Interspersing detectives among crowds greatly enhances the chance of detecting and interrupting the throwing of a missile or the firing of a gun.

The arrangement of the motorcade, if one is used, is another important consideration. The lead vehicle, a police car, maintains constant radio contact with all units in the motorcade as well as with all sector commanders who are advised of the impending arrival of the motorcade. The official visiting party is preceded, flanked, and followed by security vehicles. When weather permits, police on motorcycles are used to flank the motorcade, to cut off vehicles from entering the highway, and to control vehicular traffic.

Helicopters are used for air cover, and they are especially

useful for surveying roof-tops, tall buildings, and overpasses along the route. To avoid an accident hazard, the pilots are generally advised not to fly directly over the official party.

Security forces are briefed on what action to take in any given situation. From maps, they know the location of hospitals along the itinerary, and all equipment, medical as well as security, is kept in constant readiness. The value of this information was evident in Dallas; the wounded President was removed quickly and directly to the hospital nearest the fatal shooting.

Expert riflemen are stationed to combat snipers and an extensive arsenal of weapons is available.

An advance team (from BOSSI in New York City) is sent to every location that the official party will visit, some minutes before a dignitary's arrival to scan the area for suspicious persons. This team is critically important in performing the function of detecting not only the possible threat but even that vaguely suspicious person or vehicle that arouses the good detective to inquire further.

Photographs and dossiers of people who might constitute a danger to a visiting dignitary are distributed to security personnel who may review and refer to them as needed. These Secret Service and BOSSI files have been compiled during the intelligence gathering process, generally in connection with other investigations, and they are used because of their sudden relevance to the visit.

Buildings along routes are surveyed long before an official party passes them in order to detect possible threats as well as maintaining some minimal perfunctory supervision over people who may have firearms. Surveying buildings and neighborhoods also helps to identify mentally disturbed people who may disrupt a motorcade.

The visit of a Yassir Arafat to the United Nations may provoke such public passions as to warrant the use of really extraordinary measures like dummy motorcades, changing flight schedules, announcing false itineraries, and using look-alikes. In the latter instance, a man who looked like

Arafat was escorted, amid much fanfare, into the UN while the real Arafat was escorted through a side entrance of the building. Some hostile groups had vowed that Arafat would never speak; others threatened that he would never leave New York alive. By using the entire range of security tactics, BOSSI made Arafat's arrival, speech, and departure uneventful.

During visits like Arafat's, every movement, incident, or relevant piece of data is continuously communicated to the commanding officer of Special Services. The people there carefully record, plot, and completely investigate all information referred to them. This information from the field results in many investigations of threats, suspicious people, hazardous situations, large-scale demonstrations, and other occurrences relating to the visiting party.

The first requisite of assuring the security of a foreign visitor is a cogent grasp of that leader's government and country. Special Services' people learn the history of a visitor's country, the manner in which its leaders came to power, the identity of his entourage, and, most important of all, the nature and identity of any exile groups from that country who now live in New York City.

As a matter of routine, BOSSI closely watches the activities of exile groups to facilitate police operations in connection with demonstrations or other activities. Any given group is assigned to one or more detectives, and these detectives, chosen for their background, experience, and ability, gradually develop an impressive reservoir of knowledge. These detectives or teams are assigned a desk, which, depending upon the area being investigated, is known as the "Cuban Desk," the "Dominican Desk," or the "Middle European Desk." A great virtue of this "desk system" is that continuing responsibility is fixed for an area of investigation. More than one desk, of course, can be assigned to a team, as some groups grow inactive in an area and others become active in other areas.

The detectives assigned to an area of activity almost invariably speak the language of the group of exiles to whom they are assigned, and they have a personal familiarity with the group's culture. They are directed to widen and deepen their knowledge through study and frequent contact with the exiles. The men assigned to the Cuban Desk cover picket lines, investigate crimes, interview leaders, read Cuban newspapers and other periodicals, and generally learn as much as possible about the daily life of Cubans. The investigators will come to know various Cuban political groups and will be able to assess the probable reaction of any one of them to a given situation. They will know which groups are militant, which are moderate, and which are disbanding.

In 1962, President Osvaldo Dorticos Torrado of Cuba visited New York to attend a session of the United Nations. During his stay approximately thirty people were arrested in or near Torrado's hotel for crimes involving attempts to harm the President or a member of his party. Those arrested were disaffected Cuban exiles who BOSSI detectives recognized as belonging to anti-Dorticos factions. Penetration of President Dorticos' security screen was prevented by the familiarity the assigned detectives had with members of the newly forming pro- and anti-Castro factions in New York City, as well as with all members of the President's party.

The great residual benefit of the "desk system" is that it provides knowledgeable detectives for assignment to a visiting dignitary on short notice. No department could afford to train men precisely for occasional visits, but police in the "desk system" develop expert knowledge on exiles, and that knowledge is useful when these investigators are occasionally assigned to a state visit.

The detectives assigned to a dignitary, especially a head of state, should be able to identify immediately mentally-ill people who often have attacked heads of state to rectify a real or imagined grievance. Profiles of the possibly mentally disturbed have been developed particularly in the area of airport security. The disheveled, wild-eyed, muttering, paranoid, or object-clutching loner should be closely watched in a crowd, for many such mentally-ill people have been detected and intercepted before attacking a dignitary. Detectives should remember that

> The assassins of American presidents have been emotionally disturbed social isolates, acting on their own, without any rational expectation that they or the party and cause with which they identified themselves, could benefit from the slaying.(7)

It is vitally important to have the same team assigned to the person of a dignitary throughout the entire visit. The team, composed of men and women from BOSSI, participates in the pre-visit planning as well as the post-visit evaluation and critique. Through continued experience with visits and exposure to the public, they are able to detect the unusual or out-of-place event almost before it occurs. The team represents continuity, fixed responsibility, knowledge of assignment, and commitment to a goal. Each team member has usually participated in prior visits and has been assigned through the "desk system" to investigations related to the visit.

A number of priorities must be made during an attempt against the life of a head of state. The attacked dignitary must be safeguarded and removed from the scene of danger as quickly as possible. Safeguarding a wounded President or foreign head of state is primarily the responsibility of the Secret Service, and local police, including Special Services in New York City, play a subsidiary role. The investigation, pursuit, and arrest of a presumed assassin is, however, the responsibility of local law enforcement.(8) Special Services and the Secret Service have a concurrent responsibility for the safety of dignitaries, and each agency, while coordinating efforts, acknowledging each other's role and cooperating with one another has developed an informed system of shared authority. Safeguarding national figures, however, is a potential problem for federal and local police agencies throughout the country, and the responsibilities of each agency should be more clearly defined than they have been.

The Secret Service personnel assigned to President John F. Kennedy in Dallas, Texas on November 23, 1963 comprised less than five percent of the security force assigned to the visit. Six hundred local law enforcement people were in Dallas, while only twenty-eight Secret Service agents were assigned to the President.(9) This ratio not only illustrates the important role of local police agencies in furnishing security but also again indicates that the responsibility of each agency during and after an assassination must be assigned.

The most widely adopted method of guarding a head of state is the "concentric ring" security operation. Rings of security police radiate outward in diminishing intensity from the person guarded to cover the immediate area. These rings of guards should become successively more difficult to penetrate as one moves toward the center of the circle. The greatest concentration of manpower occurs nearest the dignitary. Security men assigned to a "concentric ring" operation must be willing to interpose themselves between the person guarded and any attacker. Recently, BOSSI agents, organized in concentric rings, prevented attackers from killing Chiang Kai-shek's son in New York by interposing themselves between the target and the attackers. The would-be assassins were quickly disarmed, and one suspect was arrested.

Uncertainty and surprise are valuable security allies. The advance announcement of the itinerary and route of a dignitary is especially dangerous, since it gives plotters the advantage of time to plan and prepare an attack. The principal dilemma of security in a free society may be represented by the conflict among the public's right to see leaders, the desire of leaders to be seen, and the anxiety of the police to provide both with maximum security.

It is important to note that the most critical phase of security is the period preceding a leader's visit. The quality of preparation and planning will determine results. Once a visitor arrives the flow of events, the pressure of the itinerary, and the excitement of the moment all militate against precautions or thoughtful action. If problems have not been anticipated before a visit, they are not likely to be solved after the visit has begun.

A dignitary's temporary residence is generally a key area in any security operation, since it is frequently the target of plotters and is the most logical site of attack. Electric generators, ventilating systems, elevator motors, and building lighting facilities should be guarded. Security forces should know the layout of the residence as well as facilities for building repairs in case damage is done. In New York City, members of the Emergency Service Division of the Police Department are trained to cope with building security problems. During Nikita Khrushchev's 1960 visit to New York, an agonizing minute occurred for BOSSI agents when the Russian leader's elevator stalled during an ascent. This painful moment was assuaged by our knowledge that the generator and cables were being covered by detectives at the moment that the elevator stalled.

No detail can be thought to be too unimportant or remote to escape consideration; no aspect of a problem should escape the grasp of police planners. For example, if a shooting occurred, it might be disastrous for police not to know the quickest route to a hospital from that precise point. The confrontation of a dignitary by a notorious enemy should be avoided as not only potentially dangerous but acutely embarrassing. A clash between contending factions of demonstrators would also be indicative of poor planning and inadequate intelligence. Flaws in planning are revealed through irretrievable and unfortunate incidents like the accident in Connecticut when a teenager's car drove through an unguarded intersection and hit President Ford's limousene. The classic example of poor security planning was Vice President Richard Nixon's visit to Lima, Peru, and Caracas, Venezuela in 1956. That chaotic trip became an international incident which fortunately did not result in injury or death to the Vice President.(10)

Before the arrival in New York City of any visiting dignitary, the potential problems of the visit are assessed by the commanding officer in Special Services. The existence and identity of groups exiled from the dignitary's country are established; their history is examined; and the volatile elements within each group are studied to detect possible threats to the visitor.

After many heads of state visited the United Nations in 1960, Police Commissioner Michael J. Murphy said:

> Information evaluated by BOSSI (Bureau of Special Services) aided immeasurably in the effective deployment of personnel throughout the entire United Nations Security Operation. Weeks before the foreign dignitaries touched United States soil, BOSSI was obtaining and screening information, helping to lay plans for history's biggest police security umbrella. The gathering and evaluation of such intelligence required a thorough check of the files, plus effective field contacts. The identity of visiting dignitaries, time and place of arrival, residences while in New York City, and complete itineraries including informal visits, sightseeing and shopping tours, were essential bits of intelligence.(11)

Commissioner Murphy also described the process of risk evaluation which involves weighing such factors as the enmity engendered by a dignitary among certain groups in New York City, the depth of their resentment, the potential for violence, and the presence of potential or likely assassins. This evaluation also involves the risks present at the residences of dignitaries, at places they plan to visit, and in automobiles to be used.

BOSSI's tedious task of carefully identifying every possible danger to a visitor has the great value of deepening its security team's awareness of risks, for the team must deal with all factors and people central to the security of the arriving guest. Special Services develops dossiers, creating priorities of security by determining who may be dangerous and who is probably a charlatan. The Bureau in its daily operations gathers a great deal of information that will be useful to a security team assigned to a visiting dignitary.

Pre-arrival preparation frequently involves investigating rumors of plots and reports of threats. No allegation is too farfetched to be checked, and no rumor is too ludicrous to be investigated. A sportsman checked into a hotel across the street from a place that President Lyndon Johnson planned to visit in New York City. The man was carrying what appeared to be a rifle in a case. A BOSSI agent investigated the man and convinced him to keep his rifle in the hotel's safe until the President arrived across the street and had departed. Another man, BOSSI learned, was threatening to kill President John F. Kennedy in June 1961, because the man had lost his life's savings in the stock market decline the previous month. BOSSI agents discreetly followed the man during the entire weekend when the President was in New York. Both cases are typical of the security investigations that invariably follow the announcement of an impending visit of a President or a dignitary.

The once voluminous central files of BOSSI, developed over years and updated constantly through new entries, formed the core of the intelligence operation. Any group or person suspected of subversion or interest in killing a public figure could be checked against these files. Not every person or organization was listed in the files, but even a negative report had the virtue of indicating the inactivity of a person or a group.

Due to recent court decisions, these central files have been greatly reduced. They are normally available to high-ranking police administrators and to the FBI, but BOSSI's liaison with other agencies declined as the uses and court ordered distribution of its data became suspect. Although contact with the Department of State and the Secret Service remains necessarily close, BOSSI's contact with military intelligence, once a thriving activity, has fallen into disuse. This break resulted mainly from the severe criticism of the Department of Defense for it surveillance, and the Counter Intelligence Corps, of civilian (or non-military) targets.

It should be noted that a distinct and permanent dichotomy existed between intelligence concerning exiles and the foreign-born and intelligence related to organized crime. The former was the province of BOSSI while the latter was the responsibility of the Organized Crime Unit that operated independently. The operations of both units rarely merged. When organized crime does venture into political activity, the responsibility of each unit may become blurred. When Joseph Colombo was shot during an Italian Civil Rights rally, the confusion as to which unit would investigate the killing was quickly resolved by assigning the investigation to the Organized Crime Unit.

A security operation requires a great deal of equipment. Automobiles, motorcycles, helicopters, and launches are used daily. Fluoroscopes are used to scan arriving packages and luggage. Detection devices such as geiger counters may be used to search large areas like the pier where the *Baltika* docked with Premier Khrushchev in 1960. Loudspeakers effectively control crowds; oxygen tanks are needed for visitors who are known cardiac risks; and high-powered rifles are required for use against snipers. Communications devices of all types, especially walkie-talkies, are used to achieve coordination and maintain contact among security forces. The staff services of the police laboratory, photographic unit, bomb squad, and other special groups within the New York City Police Department are always available to BOSSI and are frequently used.

A free society creates security risks to its leaders, because they must traditionally be accessible to the public. In America, complete protection of a President is impossible.

As J. Edgar Hoover said, "an approach to complete security would require the President to operate in a sort of vacuum, isolated from the general public and behind impregnable barriers."(12)

The American political arena is potentially an inhospitable place for any candidate or elected official, including a President. A frontier tradition of violence and the availability of firearms tend to create a national propensity for resolving problems through violent acts. In describing the roles of the President as being the head of state, Chief Executive, Commander-in-Chief, and leader of a political party, the Warren Report observed:

> In all of these roles the President must go to the people. Exposure of the President to public view through travel among the people of this country is a great and historic tradition of American life. Desired by both the President and the public, it is an indispensable means of communication between the two. More often than not, Presidential journeys have served more than one purpose at the same time: ceremonial, administrative, political.(13)

The policy of the New York City Police Department for the security of the President is illustrated in an order issued on October 12, 1964.(14) This directive, which is also applicable to visits of all dignitaries, stresses the responsibility of the police for the safety of guests, emphasizes the need for insuring that maximum security measures are taken in connection with these visits, and describes the procedures to be followed. The responsibility of the police is described in detail, but only the general outlines of an effective security operation are given in order to give police the necessary flexibility to plan each operation individually. The emphasis and thrust of the Police Department's views are heavily on the side of assuming responsibility for the safety of any guest. Abdication of responsibility would inevitably result in oversight, lapses of vigilance, and inattention to important detail, and yet avoiding responsibility for local agencies is made easier because the Department of State and the Secret Service share ill-defined areas of providing security for dignitaries. The assumption of full responsibility is the first step in an effective security operation.

The issue of presidential security was brought vividly to public attention when two attempts were made upon Gerald Ford's life within seventeen days in September 1975. The reaction to these two events was often illogical and bizarre. The need for national gun control legislation is one of the prime requisites of the President's—or anyone else's—security. Yet, after two assassination attempts against him, President Ford continued to oppose gun registration. Other proposals—using preventive detention of suspected assassins, establishing a hermetically sealed presidency, using metal detectors and other related technology—would gradually establish a self-contained, secretive national leadership.

More thoughtful proposals, like strengthening domestic surveillance and increasing infiltration of radical groups, were bound to meet stiff opposition. Yet both women who attempted to kill the President had been involved with groups that intelligence agencies normally keep under surveillance. Sara Jane Moore was involved with the radical left and black causes, and Lynnette Alice Fromme was a member of Charles Manson's "family." Although the Secret Service has a file of 47,000 names of people who are considered potential threats to the President, neither woman was listed in the file. They had both been known to the Secret Service and the California police, yet neither woman was intercepted. In a sense, Sara Jane Moore and Lynnette Fromme symbolize the most dangerous threat to a President's life: the impressionable radical of dubious mental balance and unlimited commitment to a cause.

That both women were influenced by the news media and were committed to radical causes seems clear. That investigative agencies did not have the radical groups with which both women were involved under careful surveillance also seems clear. Their interception could only have occurred through follow-up investigations which would have taken experienced detectives far beyond the range of the President's person. Determined pursuit of leads—and they existed in the case of each woman—would have resulted in their interception before they stood as close to the President as they did.

Seemingly isolated attempts against the President should not lull security forces into the belief that large, elaborate assassination plots will not arise. It seems logical to assume that terrorist groups seeking a political goal, like the creation of a Palestinian state, would view the President as an attractive, natural target for kidnapping. Other groups seeking to free "political prisoners" might conceivably terrorize a President to achieve their aims.

The Warren Report revealed some important security problems concerning American Presidents. The recommendations of the Report, which relate to the security of all dignitaries, include the following: 1. Advance agents should have more detailed instructions than they had been receiving before the assassination in Dallas. 2. Better liaison should be established with local enforcement agencies. 3. Buildings along a route should be checked. The Report infers that publication of the route is dangerous. The Commission observed that the Dallas route was published, because President John F. Kennedy was seeking maximum exposure during his Dallas trip. 4. More effective liaison and exchange of information among federal agencies are necessary. The Commission referred to the extensive FBI inquiry into Lee Harvey Oswald's background and the failure of the FBI to transmit this data to the Secret Service. 5. Uniformed officers should be instructed to face spectators and observe buildings, windows, and crowds. 6. Design of the Presidential vehicle should include security considerations. 7. The assassination of a President should be made a federal rather than a state crime. 8. The gathering of "preventive intelligence" should be stressed. 9. A cabinet-level committee should be established to advise the President on security. 10. The Secret Service should be better and more closely supervised by its parent agency, the Department of the Treasury, and should coordinate its activities with other federal agencies. 11. Reference must be continually made to FBI regulations which only recently have identified who constitutes a threat to a President's safety. 12. Better liaison among intelligence agencies should be established. 13. Electronic data-processing equipment should be used for Secret Service files. This recommendation envisions the conversion of manual files to computerized, quickly retrievable files. 14. Written plans and instructions should be prepared for local law enforcement agencies. 15. More money, people, and equipment should be allocated for the Secret Service. Two hundred and five additional agents were sought.

Although these recommendations could not, if carried out, provide absolute security for a President in a free society, the Report, nevertheless, concluded that security could be greatly improved. It is ironic, almost ten years after the Warren Report was published, that the Watergate hearings have made the personal security of Presidents and dignitaries more difficult to maintain. Within BOSSI, the security function was invariably seen and treated as providing a bodyguard service. Although opportunities existed for learning gossip about prominent people, they were never exploited. Some men on permanent assignments as security escorts for Mayor John Lindsay and Governor Nelson Rockefeller developed genuine friendships and associations beyond their official relationships. One particularly poised member of BOSSI was even made a count by a visiting prince with whom he had become acquainted. These relationships were characterized by trust and dignity, but, after Watergate, officials distrusted the security forces provided to them. One nationally prominent political figure surprised BOSSI by refusing to have a regularly detailed bodyguard assigned to him. He, or one of his staff members, had apparently concluded that a connection existed between BOSSI and Nixon's Washington and had assumed that it was possible, if not likely, that his BOSSI bodyguard was forwarding data to former BOSSI friends in the capitol. Had BOSSI learned (it did not) that this political figure was the target of an assassination attempt, it would have been virtually impossible for Special Services to provide him with the kind of security the Warren Report was recommending ten years ago.

On a local level, other security considerations include the maintenance of the history of a visit by a President or a dignitary from the initial report to the last; these reports should include a description of every significant event connected with the visit. The reports are filed in a running log of the visit, centrally kept, that includes an up-to-the-minute chronology of the itinerary. A central operations section at BOSSI, where the log is kept, directs all security at all times. Here a selection should be made of frozen areas, where maximum security is in effect and of high-risk, vulnerable places that should be closely surveyed. The itinerary of a visitor should be released on a carefully controlled basis. Different identification devices such as pins, badges, or cards should be selected, and priorities as to who receives identification badges for restricted areas are determined by BOSSI and the visitor's assistants.

Since 1865, attempts have been made on the lives of one American President out of every three. When President Kennedy was killed, the possibility of assassination was transformed—for another generation—into a ghastly reality. Security requires an unremitting professionalism. BOSSI, the organization responsible for security operations in New York City, has been effectively developed due to the consistent application of basic administrative principles; it is ably led; its personnel are carefully selected, trained, and supervised; their job roles are defined and well known; and unsuitable personnel are dismissed.

Although everyone at the Bureau realizes that absolute security is incompatible with democracy, no one assumes the inevitability of an assassin's success. Most security officials admit that a determined and well planned attempt on another's life is not likely to be stopped more than half the time. Yet the people concerned with security at BOSSI continue to develop new techniques from their experience and from their training including on-the-job orientation, classroom instruction, tours of other police agencies, and working sessions at the FBI and CIA. The success of any security operation is marked by silence, since the absence of an attempt does not make headlines. The most effective security is that which deters and frustrates assassination attempts, and BOSSI has been notably successful in providing security to hundreds of dignitaries visiting New York City. Since BOSSI was established over fifty years ago, no successful assassination has taken place in the city.

CHAPTER VI.

Labor Disputes

The role of the police during a labor dispute is delicate and complex. The safety of the public and the rights of the participants in a strike should be assured, but any semblance of police espionage or unseemly interference should be assiduously avoided. The early history of the trade union movement in American cities is filled with the kind of violence and conflict that necessarily required the police to become a peace-keeping force. The attempts of the Communist Party to infiltrate the union movement during the 1920's and 1930's served to confirm the rationale behind police involvement in the investigation of labor disputes and union activities.

The character of the Bureau of Special Services was formed quickly by its original mandate to inquire into radical activities. The investigation of subversion has been, from the time the Bureau was organized, BOSSI's raison d'etre, and the threat by communism to the union movement automatically became the concern of the Bureau.

In 1944, the Acting Commander of Special Squad #1 of the New York City Police Department wrote:

> While the (Communist) party did not make much progress in the field of national politics, its inroads into the field of labor did meet with a measure of success. The purpose behind the invasion of labor unions was to cut off the true revolutionary elements from socialism, and transform them into

communist organizations, to be used as revolutionary instruments for the conquest of power. When the Bolsheviks won power in Russia, they believed that their revolution was the first step in a world wide revolution.

They saw the road to power not in winning political elections but in mass uprisings of workers, in which strikes would play a major role. The revolutionary party had to win influence in the unions, so that its leadership would be accepted in political matters as well.

This policy is stated by (William Z.) Foster in a report to the third annual convention: "The strengthening and unification of Trade Unions for the class struggle, and the conquest of these organizations for the program of communism, are of the utmost importance to our party."(1)

As the communist threat faded, the Bureau's function of investigating communist infiltration into the union movement shifted in the 1940's to an enforcement-oriented philosophy that concentrated on the public disorder created by strikes and the potential violations of law existing in a given labor dispute. BOSSI's function evolved gradually from a political perspective on labor matters to a more practical responsibility to keep the peace and to protect the rights of union demonstrators, management, and the general public.

In the 1950's and 1960's, unions struck by creating disruptions and dislocations. They had achieved the organizational unity they sought in the early 1930's, and the focus of their disputes shifted from organizational strife to economic demands.

Labor problems for police did not change markedly. Sit-ins, lock-outs, labor goons, sabotage, and violence were replaced by boycotts, strikes, picket lines, and jurisdictional disputes. The police were still confronted with the disruption, sometimes caused illegally, of the community's life.

Labor racketering and the involvement of organized

crime with the union movement, especially in groups like the powerful Teamsters, were largely ignored by local police. Geographically and legalistically, organized crime was too overwhelming for a local unit like Special Services to investigate. Senator Estes Kefauver and Attorney General Robert Kennedy led investigations into organized crime, but the federal government and the FBI did little to sustain their assaults.

In the 1970's, middle-aged labor leaders learned that a growing number of their union members were from minority groups. Since leaders seldom part with their power willingly, and since minorities quickly perceived this reluctance, strife inevitably followed. Women, Hispanics, and blacks would not be denied representation in their unions. The white, male union leaders had not been deterred in their early battles to organize labor, and having power, they were determined to resist the new usurpers. The struggle was especially visible in the construction and produce growing industries, and again the police were expected to fulfill their responsibility to preserve the peace.

Today, urban dwellers are dependent on the efforts of hundreds of people for their daily essential needs. Some needs are luxuries, some are conveniences, and others are necessities, but almost no one can provide themselves with even a fraction of services or goods directly. In a large urban area, individuals cannot, for example, dispose of their garbage, fight major fires in their neighborhoods, or effectively treat a medical emergency in their homes. An interruption of the availability of water or electricity can become a major crisis. A strike by any of the people who supply any of these basic needs creates a major problem for police.

The impact of a strike on community life varies with the importance of the public function that is interrupted. Strikes by the military or the police would create a major crisis. Others, like those that affect an essential public service or involve a utility or a city's food supply, would, depending on their length, create major problems. Still others are inconveniences which may require a consumer to buy an alternative brand of bread or milk.

The role of the police in labor disputes is now clear and unequivocal; they preserve the peace and enforce the law evenhandedly. Police officers have to assume a neutral posture. They must preserve the rights of the parties in a dispute, and they must protect the unrepresented but important rights of the public as well.

The history of the police in labor disputes is a checkered one. The police have been criticized (and sometimes abused) for the way they have handled strikes. Some criticism may have been justified, but it is entirely possible that the neutral role that police must maintain in these disputes has led to unwarranted criticism. Donald C. Stone describes the complex role of the police during a strike:

> A brick from a striker's hand goes through a factory window: a mob of labor sympathizers turns over a police car; industrial guards posing as strikers create disorder and provide the setting for calling in militia; factory owners complain that 'sitdown' strikes are damaging private property. Events such as these in labor disputes conspire to make the job of law enforcement a difficult one. Often the public blames the police for their inability to cope with the flare-ups which accompany strikes without recognizing that the police are given an impossible task. The responsibility for failure more often may be laid at the door of the citizens of a community and its political leadership which has not possessed the courage to deal frankly and realistically with the struggle between employers and employees and the potential elements of disorder that this struggle entails.(2)

Although this account sounds somewhat dated, the essential

details remain accurate; sabotage, vandalism, criminality, extortion, coercion, and other forms of illegal behavior still frequently characterize labor disputes.

In New York City, the contract between the Social Service Employees Union and the Department of Welfare ended on December 31, 1966.(3) The Department and the Union negotiated while employees continued to work. As the negotiators reached an impasse, the Union instructed its members to report to work but to refuse to do any work assigned to them by their superiors. The tactic, first employed on June 19, 1967, was called a "work-in," because it did not technically constitute a strike, which was illegal under the Condon-Wadlin Act.(4) While the Union kept its members in Department of Welfare offices, it caused a cessation of service that was calculated to extract concessions from management at the negotiating table.

The work stoppage lasted until July 30th when the employees voted six hundred to four hundred to accept the Department's offer. Full operations resumed on Monday, July 31, 1967. During this six-week strike, numerous incidents, arrests, acts of malicious mischief, disruptions, and large-scale picketing occurred. Union membership meetings were followed by post-midnight rallies in Union Square, and the Department and the Union negotiated in an atmosphere charged with bitterness and ill-will.

The dispute was marred by a number of assaults and incidents. On June 20th a striker purposely misinformed arriving welfare clients that no money was available for them. On June 23rd strikers blocked other clients at a welfare center and refused to leave the premises. Police charged them with trespassing. Strikers made noise, interfered with on-going welfare office operations, threw eggs, blocked office entrances, slashed tires, and threatened working Department of Welfare employees as well as welfare recipients. Strikers sabotaged welfare offices by jamming locks, ransacking files, and throwing record cards on the floor. The Union seemed willing to undertake any action that might halt the operations of the Department and make management agree to the Union's contract proposals.

In 1966, the Department of Welfare spent approximately six hundred million dollars to assist 628,000 welfare clients. Essential to the disbursement of this welfare money is an electronic data-processing section located on the fifth and sixth floors of the Department's main office. These machines automatically print and address the semi-monthly checks on the first and fifteenth of each month. The Department and BOSSI knew that any sabotage of the machines would cause unbearable hardship to the city's poor. The Union seemed determined to involve the large welfare client population in its dispute in order to bring the economic vulnerability of the poor to bear on the Department, thereby creating intolerable pressure to force contractual concessions.

Clearly, some irresponsible and wilful Union members would do anything to achieve their ends, yet their efforts, although determined and energetic, were not enough to disrupt the check-forwarding process. Clients continued to receive checks for their food and rent, because Special Services realized the critical importance of the payments, anticipated the possible sabotage of the data-processing section, and took the necessary measures to preclude sabotage. Special Services was guarding the data-processing machines twenty-four hours a day three days before the work-in began.

This strike illustrates the following operations of the Bureau of Special Services in a labor dispute: 1. the value of advance intelligence. The Bureau must anticipate a work stoppage, discover the tactics to be used by labor (work-in) and by management (a lock-out). It determines vulnerable locations and guards them. Generally, an intelligence unit should anticipate all law enforcement problems posed by a strike. 2. the need to keep in close touch with negotiations. During the welfare strike information about negotiations, obtained by BOSSI, enabled the Police Department to forego any personnel assignments to the strike from the expiration of the contract on December 31, 1966 until the eve of the work-in on June 19, 1967. During the work-in BOSSI assigned its personnel according to the progress made in negotiations. When a contractual agreement was reached, all non-essential assignments were terminated. The Police Department will shift its forces and priorities on the basis of the intelligence developed by Special Services; the intelligence permits a proactive, rather than the traditional reactive response by the Department, to problems in a strike. 3. the necessity for adequate police preparations for mass picketings, rallies, and demonstrations. The planning of the Police Department is greatly assisted by the availability of a steady flow of up-to-date relevant information from BOSSI. Impromptu demonstrations which can become violent can be left un-policed if information about them is not obtained by BOSSI and referred quickly to the Police Department. 4. the value of protecting people not directly involved in a strike. In the welfare strike, fifty welfare centers at which Union members were striking, were covered by police. Serious incidents were prevented when several Union members attempted to incite or alarm arriving welfare clients. Arrests were made quickly, and disorderly conditions ended rapidly. 5. the value of protecting union people who were not striking. In the 1967 strike, approximately half of the Department of Welfare's 5000 employees did not strike. The case workers, child counselors, and home economists on strike had to be screened from those workers who refused to strike and continued work. Those working were identified by the employer by cards distributed on the basis of the past day's performance. Although the Department administered the screenings, police sometimes had to enforce procedures and deal with any disorders that resulted from the screenings.

The problems inherent in any labor dispute should be foreseen by an intelligence unit, and the necessary precautions should be taken by the police department to prevent unlawful interference with the vital functions of a community. Each strike brings its own peculiar problems, has its

own distinct impact, and causes its own singular dislocations. No formula has been devised for the policing of all
such disputes, but in New York City, the Police Department
has enunciated its policy on labor disputes and has made its
policy known to all police. The Rules and Procedures of the
Department make the following references to strikes:

> 29.0 The purpose of a peaceful, orderly labor dis-
> pute shall be deemed to be legal, unless advice is
> received to the contrary from the courts or other
> competent authority.
> 30.0 The general duties of the Police Department
> in connection with labor disputes and industrial
> unrest are to protect life and property and to main-
> tain order.
> 31.0 When notified of a strike or labor trouble in
> his precinct, the commanding officer of a patrol
> precinct or, in his absence, the desk officer shall
> direct a sergeant to the scene. The sergeant shall
> obtain the following information for the U.F. 35
> (Strike Report) and report it to the desk officer:
>> a. Name, business address and telephone
> number of employer.
>> b. Name and address of union, union local
> number, affiliation, and telephone number.
>> c. Kind of business.
>> d. Number and occupation of employees in-
> volved in the dispute.
>> e. Reason for the dispute.
>> f. Date strike declared.
>> g. Number and occupation of employees who
> will continue to work.
>> h. Trouble anticipated.
>> i. Kind of strike (sympathy, wildcat, lockout,
> secondary).
>> j. Any additional factors which would aid in

determining the number and kind of police details required.

33.0 The manner in which a labor dispute is to be handled is largely at the discretion of the patrol precinct commander. He shall arrange for proper police coverage. He must bear in mind that the best police work is that which prevents unlawful action by any of the contending parties. He shall interview the owners of the business involved or their representatives and the union officials and picket captains or leaders. He shall inform them of their rights and limitations in connection with the dispute and notify or warn them:

a. That force or violence will not be tolerated.

b. That the law will be enforced with strict impartiality.

c. That the rights of the public using the streets and sidewalk will be protected.

d. That unlawful conditions or acts which lead to disorder will be prevented.

e. Against the employment of professional bullies and thugs.

f. Against activities of professional agitators.

g. That no parties to the dispute may use language or manner of address which is offensive to public decency or may provoke violence.

h. That the rights of striking employees to conduct orderly picketing will be fully protected in accordance with the circumstances and conditions existing at the location.

i. Of the number of pickets to be permitted.

j. That striking employees may picket in the vicinity or in front of the place of employment to:

1. Persuade those-still employed to strike.

2. Persuade those considering employment not to do so.

3. Inform customers about the labor dispute.

34.0 If necessary, the patrol precinct commander shall make a survey to determine:

a. Location, size of the plant, number of exits and entrances, loading platforms, etc.

b. Other buildings or locations which might be affected by the dispute.

c. Time of arrival and departure of employees who will not strike.

d. Transit facilities and routes used.

e. Entrances and exits used by employees.

f. Meal periods for employees, and whether they eat on the premises.

g. Exits, entrances, and routes used by employees during meal periods.

h. Time when merchandise is to be received or shipped.

i. Special hazards or other conditions affecting police duty.

36.0 Members of the force assigned to locations affected by a labor dispute shall be instructed to be strictly impartial and be alert to prevent:

a. Violations of law such as assaults, coercion, or unlawful interference with persons or property.

b. Physical contact or violence between factions.

c. Assembly of crowds that tend to intimidate persons or hinder passage to or from such places.(5)

These passages furnish clear guidelines to the Department's policy and indicate the need of police to support this policy with a cogent grasp of relevant laws. Faithful adherence to this policy usually assures minimal coverage of a strike, but the more sophisticated aspects of labor disputes require much deeper study.

In labor disputes, the detectives of an intelligence unit should be familiar with the legal rights of employees and employers as well as with the legal restrictions upon them.

Employees have the general right to join or not to join a union. However, when a majority agree to recognize a union, a closed shop is created, and any employee who fails to join the union with the majority may be discharged by the employer. An employee may quit working at any time but may not break a contract or, by quitting, endanger life or property. Employees may engage in lawful strikes, picket in an orderly fashion, and participate in the collective bargaining process.

On the other hand, employees may not abandon work if leaving it endangers life and property. They may not congregate in unreasonable numbers or obstruct entrances to the place of employment. They may not damage property, assault anyone, use offensive language, or engage in disorderly conduct. They are further enjoined from carrying signs on which false statements and claims appear.

Employers may generally hire anyone they wish to employ, subject to the limitations imposed by labor laws, the Wagner Act, and Fair Employment Practice Laws. They retain at their discretion the right to discharge employees, but firing cannot be based solely on the grounds of an employee's union activities. Usually a union contract describes the causes and conditions under which employees may be discharged. Employers have the same rights as employees to inform the public of a dispute and to state their views of it. Discrimination on the basis of race, sex, age, religion and nationality is proscribed by federal law.

Employers must abide by the terms of any contract they sign or suffer legal consequences. They may not discriminate against any employee because of union affiliation. The laws further forbid the employment of bullies or thugs to break a strike, and employers may not use force or intimidation against employees to break a strike. Management is also legally prohibited from spying on those engaged in union activities.

The wildcat subway stoppage in New York City in 1957, when the Motormen's Benevolent Association tried to organize motormen in a union separate from the Transport Workers Union, featured charges of Transit Authority spying on the motormen's group during union meetings. A microphone which had been hidden at the meetings was shown on television by Frank Zelano, President of the Motormen's Benevolent Association. In retrospect, this illegal electronic spying seems to foreshadow Watergate, for it was implied then that the microphone had been planted by official city agencies. The dispute was no simple management vs. labor problem but involved an alliance between the recognized union (the Transport Workers Union) and the administrators of the city in opposition to a rump organization. The source of the bug was never discovered, and no prosecution followed the discovery.

Finally, management may not require people to join a company union as a condition of employment or to give up union membership to retain employment. They may not discourage employees from joining a union, and they may not refuse to bargain collectively. Under Fair Employment Practices Laws, employers cannot discriminate against their employees or applicants for jobs.

American courts have frequently addressed themselves to questions arising from labor disputes, and some general principles have emerged from these decisions. Generally, peaceful picketing is lawful, and picketing without a strike is no more unlawful than a strike without pickets. Picketing of a shop where employees are not on strike is permitted whether the shop is unionized or not. Further, the police may limit the number of pickets as long as that limitation is reasonable and based on fact.

Mass picketing is legal. However, when a large crowd organizes itself into formations, obstructs sidewalks by lying down on them, blocks building entrances, shouts, and uses loud speakers, the crowd is breaking the law. Courts have held that picketing the homes of employees to compel them to pay union dues is unlawful and may be coercion. In an important decision, the courts held that picketing by a black organization to compel the employment of blacks was in itself a labor dispute, subject to the rights and limitations of such a dispute.

The courts have expressed themselves on the content and nature of signs that may be used in labor disputes. Carrying signs stating that a strike exists where none actually does constitutes disorderly conduct. Using trucks carrying signs that advertise a strike was held to be a violation of U.S. ordinances. The courts have also held that picketing the home of an employee who has not gone on strike or carrying a sign that states that an employee is a "scab" or a "strike-breaker" constitutes disorderly conduct. Only people who replace striking workers may be referred to as "scabs" or "strike-breakers." They may not be applied to non-striking employees.(6)

Most detectives assigned to the approximately three hundred labor disputes investigated each year by the Bureau of Special Services have had a great deal of experience in labor-management relations. Their experience is essential, because most of their inquiries depend on interpersonal relations in which trust, integrity, and confidence play a major part. Police also need to know the internal methods and operations of a union, its history, and the personality and character of its leaders. Conditions within an industry, the history of past negotiations, the temperament of management, and the relative merits of the offers and demands made all tend to affect the outcome of a labor dispute.

The proper role of the police is generally established in the passage from *Municipal Police Administration* quoted earlier in this book. Yet exceptions occur, especially during a police strike which can wreak havoc with the sentiments of the intelligence unit assigned to monitor the dispute. Fortunately, during the 1971 police strike in New York City, the patrol officers struck while detectives, including BOSSI detectives, continued to work, because they did not belong to the patrol officers' union. A monitoring agent's foremost responsibility is to keep abreast of the progress and developments of negotiations during a strike and to advise his superiors as to what can be anticipated. Monitoring is widely regarded by union and management as a perfectly legitimate enterprise and should present no problems even when it involves police monitoring a police strike.

A labor dispute is much like an iceberg; only a fraction of it, perhaps a list of demands, is visible, while the substance, the negotiations, are generally not visible to the public. Frequently, a union leader confronts management with a series of extreme demands. A strike results, not because he had seriously hoped to see his demands met but because a militant faction within his union may itself be demanding extreme concessions from management. To prove to all of his members that he represents their best interest, a union leader may sound as fanatical as Hitler. That a union leader's apparent fanaticism is only the public tip of labor-management negotiations is an integral part of an investigator's knowledge.

A police department, in allocating its resources and establishing priorities, wants to know whether a strike will occur and how long it may last. The department will want to consider the possibilities of violence and breaches of the law. Orders must be printed, vulnerable locations must be guarded; ground rules for picketing must be established. Timothy J. Walsh has said, "An effective police department will know through its own sources when labor trouble is developing in its area."(7) He adds that labor disputes have a potential for violence when:

1. There is bitterness between strikers and employer, 2. Violence is deliberately employed as a tactic, and 3. An incident or misunderstanding sparks violence.

The following information, according to Walsh, must be obtained by police:

1. Exact time strike is to begin, expiration of contract etc., 2. The parties to the dispute., 3. Issues involved, 4. Operations in event of strike, 5. What function stops, who works if there is a strike, 6. Employers estimate as to who will work, 7. Working hours, 8. Crime hazards—-payroll deliveries, vulnerable points, 9. Internal security used by employer, 10. Employer's plans for internal security, 11. Identity and phone numbers of union officials, 12. Equipment to be used by union sound trucks etc, 13. Whether mass picketing is planned, 14. Whether union will use caravan or motorcade, 15. Tactics of harassment that might be used by union, 16. Whether boycott, "wives' march," or similar tactic contemplated, 17. Location of union command post, 18. Any public statements by union officials on violence, 19. Whether emergency feeding of strikers is required, and 20. What strike funds are available for strikers.(8)

These twenty items serve to illustrate two important segments of the pre-strike investigatory process: 1. The breadth of the process is such that no list can expect to exhaust the possibilities or anticipate all future difficulties in a dispute and 2. The items listed serve as an excellent guide to the police administrator who must cope, without previous experience, with a major labor problem.

The Bureau of Special Services will rarely inquire into a labor matter involving less than a hundred employees. The size of the employed group generally distinguishes the potentially important strike from the unimportant one. Most labor controversies, even of larger groups than a hundred employees, can be handled at the precinct level. Critical industries and service unions are carefully watched at BOSSI by means of a suspense file of cards. Some time before the expiration of a union contract, a BOSSI investigator will automatically receive a card on that union and its history. The card enables the investigator to initiate further inquiries into the approaching negotiations. Each case is handled by the detective who either handled the union's last dispute or by another investigator who has had contact with the union, with management, or perferably with both. With the union and management, the BOSSI investigator learns when negotiators are to meet, and he himself begins to establish a friendly, professional relationship with both parties that must develop mutual confidence and trust before bargaining begins. The detective must be trusted by labor and management in order to receive information on the true status of future negotiations. He can then alert the Police Department during negotiations to prepare for possible plant closings, demonstrations, and picketing.

The formal expiration date of a labor contract is not always the signal for a strike if no agreement has been reached. In some industries, negotiators agree to "stop the clock" during bargaining; union members continue to work with the understanding that the new contract will be retroactive to the expiration date of the old contract. Other unions faithfully adhere to a policy of "no contract, no work."

The actual start of a strike is the critical moment for a police department, for the first public clash between employer and employees can result in violence if both parties are not legally restrained by police. Picket lines must be policed, vulnerable locations must be guarded, and, based on information supplied by investigators, the appropriate responses to the dispute must be made by the police department. Special Services operates on the principle of economy: maximizing the protection of labor, management, and the public while minimizing the assignment of its personnel.

During a strike, detectives follow the progress of negotiations closely and carefully assess the bargaining climate. They know that an impasse may result in violence. During a deadlock, the greatest secrecy is maintained, and investigators are pressured by the police department to verify the status of the talks. During a critical deadlock, the effectiveness of the intelligence agent meets its most severe test, for the agent must obtain information from the negotiators that is not available to the press. His success at learning whether movement has been made toward an agreement may free large numbers of police for other duty, while lack of progress may involve the assignment of emergency tours and involve overtime costs.

Throughout a strike, the objective of Special Services is to keep top administrators in the Police Department informed of developments. These administrators should possess all of the relevant facts concerning a developing labor problem in order to solve it rationally and objectively. Detectives telephone their reports to the Operations Center, the nerve center of the Police Department, and later written narratives are filed. The Police Department consequently not only receives up-to-the-minute intelligence but eventually also has a full and accurate history of a dispute.

Once a labor agreement is reached—remarkably the bargaining process does invariably result in agreement—steps can be taken to insure an orderly transition to resuming normal work. For police, the impact of the transit strike of 1966 was softened, because it occurred during the holidays. However, the responsibility of the police during the closing and resumption of transportation service was as critical as it was during the strike itself when people and traffic had to be rerouted, especially at commuting times.

Special Services is well aware that its function is not to spy on either labor or management but, rather, to convey all available intelligence to police administrators who must make decisions. That a complex city like New York survived a paralyzing transit strike is a reminder that "the way in which industrial strikes are handled will contribute in a major way to the public welfare and the public regard for its own police."(9)

CHAPTER VII.

Liaisons and Policy

> The main weakness in our defense against crime
> is the poor exchange of information among police
> departments.(1)
>
> The Commission has concluded that there was
> insufficient liaison and coordination of informa-
> tion between the Secret Service and other Federal
> agencies necessarily concerned with Presidential
> protection.(2)
>
> Effective cooperation among law enforcement
> agencies is a must today if citizens are to be pro-
> vided the protection they deserve.(3)

Whether it is investigating the status of aliens or subversive groups, protecting a national or international dignitary,
or monitoring a labor dispute, Special Services is inevitably
brought within the operational orbits of other federal and
state agencies. Cooperation among agencies can provide an
opportunity to improve law enforcement, and police have
often coordinated their efforts while avoiding the dangers of
uncoordinated and parallel inquiries. In addition to supple-
menting functions and exchanging data, police departments
can establish operational cooperation among other agencies,
and as the President's Commission on Law Enforcement and
Administration of Justice stated:

> There is continuing need for coordination between
> the law enforcement agencies of the Federal Gov-

ernment on the one hand, and State and local intelligence units on the other.(4)

This coordination has resulted in the creation of multi-agency task forces that are designed to attack the problems posed by organized crime and narcotic trafficking. These forces typically included federal, state, and local agents working together under supervisory ranks that included representatives from all three governmental levels. The task forces represent one of the most imaginative approaches undertaken by law enforcement professionals to attack problems that have been defeating the criminal justice system for decades.

Although the task forces were not involved with the direct concerns of BOSSI, the New York City Police Department does maintain a strong liaison with the federal government. The presence of missions representing over a hundred members of the United Nations, as well as the organization itself, would inevitably establish channels of communication between local and federal agencies. In addition to the presence of other consulates and missions, the frequent arrival of diplomats and visits of heads of state and other dignitaries make this liaison the area of greatest contact between the federal government and the New York City Police Department.

In addition to the approximately twelve hundred annual contacts involving diplomats, consuls, and missions, the Bureau of Special Services serves as a clearing house for all Department of State business with the Police Department, including such delicate matters as the investigation of a crime in which diplomatic immunity becomes the controlling factor. Special Services may assign a patrolman to cover an ambassador's residence, to investigate a theft at a mission, or to discover a planned demonstration at an embassy where the participants will employ some unlawful act. Any inquiry into a complaint or allegation made by a foreign mission to the Department of State usually involves the Police Department and consequently Special Services.

Problems requiring the attention of the police are literally endless, and contact with the Bureau is made daily by phone, by letter, or in person. Diplomatic relations fortunately have been long characterized by a spirit of cooperation and amicability.

The Bureau of Special Services probably most closely resembles the Federal Bureau of Investigation in its investigative responsibilities and methods of operation. Both deal with subversive elements; both undertake security inquiries; both maintain an elaborate intelligence apparatus concerned with the activities of criminal or potentially criminal groups.

That the functions and responsibilities of the FBI and BOSSI are similar create a danger of duplicated effort. This danger is enhanced by the jealousy and secretiveness that generally mark relations between two investigative units. This troublesome potential has been eased by the development of effective liaison and a free-flowing interchange of information. The permanent assignment of an agent to serve as a liaison between the FBI and the Police Department has resulted in a flow of information to the federal level that would be difficult to obtain without the liaison.

The FBI is charged with the responsibility for investigations in connection with the security program of the federal government under Executive Order #10450 issued on April 27, 1953.

The FBI conducts full field investigations of all federal employees "to insure that employment and retention of employment. . . .is clearly consistent with the interests of national security." The full field investigation involves: 1. National agency check, 2 Verification of place and date of birth, 3. Citizenship, 4. Education, 5. Employment, 6. Military service, 7. References, 8. Police and criminal records, 9. Neighborhood investigation, 10. Credit record, 11. Foreign travel, 12. Foreign connections, 13. Organizations, and 14. Other factors.(5)

Special Services performs the same function as the FBI, on the municipal level, when it conducts the security check part of the investigation that the Police Academy makes into the background of prospective city employees. The cooperation and aid of an agency such as BOSSI makes the conduct of such an inquiry much easier for the local employer.

The security of the President, the Vice-President, and their families is the responsibility of the Secret Service and, during their visits to New York City, of the Bureau of Special Services. As we have seen, the techniques involved in presidential security require the closest possible cooperation between these two agencies. Because of its limited size, the Secret Service must concentrate on guarding the person of the visiting national leader and on exploring only the most sensitive investigations. In a large city, only the local investigative unit and police department would have enough personnel to investigate local threats, cover the route of the visitor, guard his residence, etc.

Because the Bureau not only screens all city employees but also examines the backgrounds of many federal and state workers, it works with the New York State Police, the military intelligence the investigative agencies of other cities, and many other organizations within the federal government. The Bureau's cooperation centers on the exchange of information on subversive people or groups active within New York City, who may have been active in other parts of the country.

The relationships established through these contacts ultimately encompassed entire police departments, and inquiries were greatly facilitated by an almost nation-wide network of cooperation and coordination. The liaison function of Special Services grew as the need for it expanded. In retrospect, one had only to look at the number of agencies involved in the investigation of subversive activities, the protection of foreign dignitaries, and the background inquiries of public employees to recognize the power law enforcement agencies were acquiring. During the late 1960's and early 1970's, coordinated investigations involved all levels and branches of federal, state, and local governments.

The Watergate hearings and the related disclosures of criminal activity by the CIA, FBI, and the military have aroused public distrust of coordinated investigative work by law enforcement agencies. All intelligence-gathering activity has seemingly been attacked as invasions of privacy, and many needed investigative operations have been dismounted because of the resentments engendered by the criminal excesses of intelligence agencies. They had breached the public trust and the law, and the price of that criminality was the dismantling of much of the agencies' coordinated investigations. The intelligence failures inherent in the two assassination attempts made against President Ford in 1975 may be indicative of public over-reaction to Watergate. It appeared that coordinated intelligence- gathering work had been seriously crippled.

In the 1930's and 1940's, it was generally accepted that aliens constituted a potentially subversive element in American society, and as a result, the arrest of aliens was brought to the attention of BOSSI, since it was charged with investigating subversive groups. The security fever that relocated many Japanese into camps during World War II also rendered other nationalities suspect. An alien, arrested for any crime including jaywalking, was considered a potential security problem, and it was believed essential that BOSSI be notified by the arresting unit so that the Bureau could check its records for evidence of the alien's other possible activities.

During World War II, national preoccupation with security was directed not only at the nationals of our military enemies but to other aliens as well. Communist front organizations like the American Committee for the Protection of the Foreign Born contributed to national xenophobia. This organization, repeatedly cited as subversive and communist, was described as being "effectively under the management, direction and supervision, and controlled by members and representatives of the Communist Party."(6)

Since the United States Immigration and Naturalization Service had to be notified of the arrest of an alien in order to establish the alien's status in the country, a liaison was developed between the Service and BOSSI. That every arrested alien should be investigated resulted from the theory that many aliens were subversives engaged in radical activities. Since BOSSI was responsible for investigating radical activities, it could undertake an inquiry into the background of an arrested alien, notify the Immigration Service, and clear up the case without involving other Police Department units.

This administrative anachronism of dealing with an arrested alien has survived to the present day, although the process has been refined and streamlined. Today, the process is routine and almost perfunctory. When an alien, for any reason, is arrested, the desk officer of the precinct where the arrest occurred prepares a card that is forwarded to Special Services. A detective notifies the Immigration Service of the arrest, checks the files, and if a criminal record is found, forwards it to the Immigration Service which makes a final disposition of the case.

The primary responsibility for investigating aliens, especially as it relates to deportable crimes, now lies with the United States Immigration and Naturalization Service. Today only the administrative mechanics are used at Special Services when an alien is arrested, and little real investigation is conducted on the approximately twelve hundred aliens arrested for all crimes every year in New York City.

As America continued to attract uprooted people from all over the world, immigration officials estimated that as many as one million illegal aliens were in New York City in 1975. The hospitality usually extended to the foreign-born was frayed by an economic recession that left nine percent of the population unemployed. Competition for scarce jobs was intensified by the intrusion of aliens into the crowded labor market. Unscrupulous employers have proved very willing to exploit the aliens in non-skilled, non-union jobs, and it would seem that a new urgency on the federal level will arise to detect and to investigate these aliens. Perhaps, as in the 1940's, new liaisons among federal, state and local agencies will be forged, not only to deport alien workers, but also to protect employment opportunities for American citizens. As these liaisons are made, a national network for intelligence may be formed to create the same kind of Big Brother governmental agency that was uncovered in the FBI and CIA after the Watergate hearings.

The fear of Orwell's Big Brother haunts every free society, and rightly so. The price of liberty is constant vigilance, but that vigilance cannot be restricted only to the protection of human rights. The vigilance must be extended to include the protection of society and its institutions. Although the United States was founded as a result of revolution, it discarded revolution for evolutionary development. This development is not unique to American culture, but, as a people, Americans have been loath to admit desertion of revolution, because they suspect that it involves a repudiation of our Founding Fathers and their philosophy. Nevertheless, legislators have supported evolutionary national growth by creating laws and statutes against anarchy, treason, espionage, and other forms of subversive, revolutionary activity.

A democratic society's right to protect itself is self-evident. That this protection cannot include measures that alter the society in ways that make the society totalitarian or oppressive is also widely recognized and generally accepted. A democratic society must therefore strike a delicate balance between taking the necessary measures of self-protection and retaining the basic characteristics that these steps are intended to protect. In democracy, the rights of citizens must be balanced against the preservation of society; in a totalitarian society, no such balance exists.

The imperative need for information on subversive activities must, in a democracy, be subordinated to the philosophical, legal, and ethical principles that guide society. The United States is a nation of laws, and in considering how to protect the nation, people must consider that the ultimate repository of the nation's beliefs is the law. Every agency of government must adhere to its legal mandate. The legal foundation of the Bureau of Special Services is the mandate to the New York City Police Department to preserve the peace, prevent crime, protect life and property, and enforce the laws. Some of these responsibilities are delegated by the Department to sub-units like Special Services which, in discharging its daily functions, must operate within the guidelines of written law.

The work of Special Services is intended to help the Police Department realize its mission, and, to do so, the Bureau must thoroughly know the society in which the police operate. For example, the Bureau knows from experience that any rise in transit fares results in opposition and demonstrations. In 1972, after a subway fare increase, eleven people were arrested for chaining subway gates open at the 34th Street and Sixth Avenue IND station, allowing approximately five hundred people to enter the subway platform without paying their fares. In 1975 the transit fare was increased again. In late August, a meeting was called which drew militant leftists, radical unionists, Puerto Rican Nationalists, Harlem groups, and other opponents of the fare increase. Disruptions of the transit service were demanded, and sites, centrally crowded stations, were announced where groups would crash exit gates to allow riders to enter subway platforms without paying fares. To the Police Department, these illegal disruptions endanger public safety and halt or stall public transportation. To uphold the law effectively, the police needed to know where and how disruptions are planned, how many subway stations will be affected, how many people will be breaking the law, and what strategy should be adopted to arrest the demonstrators while protecting the safety of bystanders. The police need intelligence. They can no longer cope with events like subway disruptions on an ad hoc basis or by reacting to each disruption as it occurs. If they did, a Keystone Cops comedy of chases and pratfalls would ensue. A modern police department, dealing as it must with finite resources and infinite responsibilities, needs advance information which is obtainable only through an intelligence unit.

The ability of the police to uphold the law is intimately connected with the quality and amount of advance information it receives in New York from the Bureau of Special Services. The record of the Bureau illustrates the efficiency that any unit should achieve to function effectively, and further, defines the activities that properly fall within the purview of a police intelligence operation.

These activities of the Bureau are limited by law in the Penal Code, the City Charter, the Code of Criminal Procedure, and the Rules and Procedures of the Police Department. The definitions of emotional words like "subversion," "treason," "communist," "fascist," and "nationalist," are also conditioned and limited by the law. The consistent reference to the law—matching investigative activities against the Penal Code—is the greatest single safeguard an intelligence unit can have against abuse and against exceeding the legal limitations imposed upon it.

Of necessity, intelligence agencies are secretive organizations that often perform beyond the range of public scrutiny. Secrecy permits a great deal of working freedom but creates grave potential for abuse. The Hoover Commission, in considering the functions of intelligence agencies of the federal government, recommended in 1955 that a watchdog committee be appointed to oversee the operations of the Central Intelligence Agency. The committee was never formed, and one can only speculate whether the Bay of Pigs would have occurred and whether some of the Watergate revelations would have been made had some committee been checking CIA. Two decades later it seems certain that the Hoover Commission's recommendation will be finally adopted by Congress.

Special Services is subjected to daily contact with the highest ranking members of the Police Department. The reports of the Bureau, averaging more than two a day, are sent directly to the men who bear the ultimate responsibility for the operations of the Police Department. Additionally, the Police Department, can as it has in the past, appoint as the head of the Bureau, an exceptionally capable career officer who may start as a captain and be promoted several times up to the rank of Deputy Chief. One man consequently can lead the unit for a long period of time without shifting assignments within the unit, or upsetting the organizational table. These two controls—the daily review of operations by higher authority and the selection of the best available officer to command—are effective methods of insuring the operational integrity of an intelligence unit.

The volume of work imposes its own restrictions and integrity upon a unit. Material and personnel resources must be allocated on the basis of priorities and, as long as the work exceeds the unit's ability to get it done, needless, probably unproductive, investigation is not undertaken. A policy of deliberately undermanning an intelligence unit, short of crippling the operation, may be the most effective way of restricting the unit to its mandate. Administrators are generally tempted to make optimum use of their resources; if they have an unlimited access to men and money, administrators will be tempted to use them for operations that may not be covered by the unit's mandate.

Special Services does not have the reputation of other intelligence units that have engaged in witchhunts. Despite vigorous attacks by many groups that have been investigated, smear campaigns have failed. The occasional charge that BOSSI (or the "Red Squad" as some critics have dubbed it) engages in "Gestapo" or "N.K.V.D." tactics is readily proved false by the public record. Over the past five years, BOSSI has been subjected to a crossfire of law suits and criminal trials. Not one trial has revealed a breach of law by the Bureau; its record in court would seem to indicate that the Bureau has adhered to its mandate.

The policy that guides the operations of Special Services

vis-a-vis the New York City Police Department, the society it serves, and the elements it investigates, is basically sound. Over the years that policy has developed within legal restrictions. Adventurism has been meticulously avoided, and the unit has been notably resistant to flattery and fashionable causes. An investigative agency is always provided with popular and convenient targets that would result in enthusiastic public support. In the 1950's Special Services was tempted by the publicity of Senator Joseph McCarthy to concentrate its work on the radical left, and, in the 1960's, it was pressured to investigate the American Nazi Party of George Lincoln Rockwell. Although Special Services investigated both groups, neither group became the sole target of the Bureau. Unlike BOSSI, the FBI, during much of its history, was tempted to pursue its investigations of communists while largely ignoring the growing, largely ill-defined illegality of organized crime.

The stable growth of the Bureau is all the more remarkable because of the absence of material and guides on the development of an intelligence unit. Law enforcement literature deals with many aspects of police work, but intelligence is one endeavor that has generally been ignored. Until recently, the field of police intelligence has been abandoned to the fiction writers, and, consequently, most police departments in the United States seem to be totally ignorant of the value and uses of an intelligence unit.

Even the most learned and prestigious recent studies— *The President's Crime Commission Report, The Warren Report,* studies of the International Association of Police Chiefs on various police departments, and *Police Administration,* by O. W. Wilson—barely refer to the operation of an intelligence organization. They may have perpetuated the belief that intelligence units cannot be very useful. The development of Special Services into a model intelligence unit is significant not only because of its value to the New York City Police Department but also because it serves as a possible model for other police departments.

The internal organizational shape of Special Services is amorphous; the unit has been allowed to develop flexibly and organically. Within the Bureau's operations, the daily shift in emphasis, occasioned by the increasing activities of one group and the decreased movements of another, requires instant response and adjustment.

Personnel selection procedures are sound, because they have consistently produced the kind of detective who functions most effectively in the Bureau. Requirements for employment are realistic and achievable, and tests are objective.

The unit's reliance on the "desk system" develops experts and assures coverage of areas determined to be important. Desk assignments, however, require periodic review, because one desk may suddenly become inactive and personnel assigned to that desk would be underutilized. They should be assigned to new areas. For example, the investigators of the Fair Play for Cuba Committee, a pro-Castro communist group, became inactive and were reassigned after Lee Harvey Oswald was killed. The association of Oswald's name with the Committee proved fatal to the organization; the group simply expired as its members scattered.

The offices of Special Services have wisely been located away from normal police installations. Although no particular secret is made of BOSSI's location in lower Manhattan, its site is conducive to normal, uninterrupted business-office operations. The location keeps the office removed from the public and the press at Police Headquarters, the Police Academy, and other installations. There is an advantage in allowing target groups to discover the major operational site of Special Services. These groups are sometimes lulled into thinking that they have discovered the source of investigation and consequently begin to focus their attentions on operations. One target group spent a great deal of time film-ing people entering and leaving Special Services offices, while BOSSI detectives, investigating the group, conducted their undercover operation from a small, clandestine cover elsewhere in the city.

Administrative controls have evolved over the years as need arose; they are useful and valid. Experience and obser-vation have demonstrated, for example, that the record files are efficient because of the speed and consistency of re-trieval. Responsibility for the source of the data in any document on file is fixed. It is a simple matter to determine who investigated a given matter years after the investigation.

The question of the place of an investigative unit on the police organizational chart is frequently raised. Until re-cently, and intermediate unit, Central Office Bureaus and Squads (COBS) existed below the Chief of Detectives and above Special Services. COBS channelled to and from BOSSI all relevant matters originating in a variety of head-quarters staff units of the Detective Division and the office of the Chief of Detectives. COBS proved to be an unnecessary organization and was eventually abolished.

On an organizational chart, an intelligence unit belongs directly under the highest authority in a police department; it should report directly to the Chief of Police. The unit's function is to keep top police management informed of po-tentially criminal activity so that a metropolitan police strategy can be quickly devised to counteract the activity and to protect the community. Any organizational delay in this function (like that caused by COBS) is not productive.

The selection of the commander of an intelligence unit is one of the most important decisions a Chief of Police can make. The commander should have the intelligence and political sophistication to be able to distinguish between radicalism and criminality. He must be strong enough to pursue unpopular goals or to veto his superiors when they consider unwise policies. Although a commanding officer should be reliable and competent, his integrity must be unimpaired. It if is not, the commander can become a pawn of a police chief or a mayor. A commanding officer must be able to subordinate his personal gains to the principles of law. He must be especially honest when dealing with possible corruption in or infiltration of the unit. Intelligence agencies are prime targets for infiltrators, and anyone doubting the dangers of infiltration has only to read the disclosure that Harold Adrian Russell Philby, a senior intelligence officer in the British intelligence service, had been a Russian spy for thirty years.

The wide free-wheeling operations of an agency like CIA, with virtually unlimited resources, few external controls over operations, secrecy surrounding appropriations, and a global area of operation clearly calls for the imposition of controls. In New York City, the Bureau of Special Services has a very limited budget, investigates only activities that are actually or potentially clearly criminal, and is supervised and controlled very closely by the top administrators in the Police Department. Despite Special Services' limited operation, controls are needed on a local level, for the public cannot rely on a succession of honorable Chiefs of Police and commanders of the unit to control the unit's integrity.

Law enforcement agencies, as a sub-branch of the executive branch of the government are generally subjected to judicial review only. If the workings of the unit do not lead to the courts, then the activities of an investigative agency remain shrouded in secrecy. The legislative branch of government proposes laws and procedures for police to follow but rarely inquires into the administration of these laws. The failure of legislators to consider the administration of law creates a dangerous void for investigative units on the federal, state, and local level. A legal control like a monitoring committee is needed not only for the activities of the CIA and FBI but also for the operations of Special Services.

The files of Special Services have been reduced substantially in recent years as a result of court actions. Although there was never a pejorative connotation to the existence of a reference in these files (it was the nature of the reference that mattered to police), much useful information has been eliminated as a result of this purge. For example, a reference to a complaint that a person or organization was engaged in criminal activities is deleted when Special Services proves the complaint false. However, every future complaint about the same person or organization must be meticulously reinvestigated since the data on which to base a filing of the matter is now destroyed.

The files of Special Services should remain under the control of the Bureau. It is repeatedly suggested that files should be kept in a central police repository for quick referral. However, files are virtually organic on a local level, in that they are constantly being initiated, changed, or deleted, and the full significance of any entry can only be appreciated by an experienced reference clerk. Local files should be maintained even though a central data bank may be established. That the Freedom of Information Act, giving citizens access to governmental files, has been passed, may hasten the establishment of national police files as the public's power of review is strengthened and the fear of intelligence files diminishes.

Special Services should not be combined with any other intelligence unit which may administer internal discipline within the Police Department. In 1967 a study (8) of the New York Police Department, conducted by the International Association of Chiefs of Police, recommended the organization of an Inspectional Services Bureau comprised of an Intelligence Division to investigate organized crime and subversive activities; an Inspections Division to determine whether police objectives were being met within established policy outlines; an Internal Affairs Division to be responsible for internal discipline; and an Administrative Vice Division to oversee the effectiveness of police operations against vice.

These recommendations were generally implemented over time, but requiring Special Services detectives to spy on other police to discover corruption would have rendered the Bureau ineffective. Being responsible for internal investigations within the Police Department, Special Services would have engendered the hostility of the police who would naturally be reluctant to help a unit identified with spying on them. The present effectiveness of the Bureau is due in no small measure to the cooperation and willingness of police in the field. No internal inspection unit concerned with discipline should expect to receive help from police it may have under surveillance. Special Services successfully resisted the effort to make it responsible for internal police investigations which are now handled by the Internal Affairs Division.

Clandestine operations should be kept separate from the overt workings of the unit. There is always the temptation to ask an undercover agency for a specific piece of data. To obtain that information, the agent may endanger the long range effectiveness and secrecy of his operation. Executives are frequently tempted to sacrifice long established covert operations for immediate gains, and this temptation should be resisted if the safety of the agents and the effectiveness of the unit are to be maintained. Any efforts to lower the barriers between overt and covert operations will ultimately harm both.

Finally, the recruitment base for Special Services should be broadened to include the entire police department. The U.F. 57 process is in danger of atrophying because of high level resistance and suspicion of it. It is too anonymous and egalitarian a process to suit some. Every member of a force should have the opportunity to be reviewed for assignment to the intelligence unit. Open recruitment is good for the morale of the unit and the police force. The validation by police officers of this process, which is a formal request for transfer to the unit, is vitally important.

Probably riots will continue to erupt sporadically over the urban scene for the next few years at least. During the summer of 1975 disorders occurred in Detroit to remind police of the volatility of the ghetto. In New York City people retaliated against a police killing of a young man by directing a police officer to a booby trap where a bomb exploded in his face. The poor remain sensitive to situations they perceive as injustices.

If the democratic order of society is to be maintained, police should contain violence and terrorism within manageable limits, while other social forces move to eradicate the conditions that create rioting and temporary chaos. In a sense, the police should fight a holding action while social changes occur. That police will continue to play a defensive role seems clear, for the underlying causes of civil disorder, such as unemployment and racism, have not been ameliorated. Seven years after the appearance of the report of the President's Commission on Civil Disorders, little progress has been made to attack the serious social ills described in that report.

Mayors of cities facing urban riots are often tempted to ask for the National Guard as a reinforcement for local police. The National Guard has not been a suitable peace-keeping force with any long range prospect of success. The National Guard should be called only as a last resort, and then its role should be recognized as the imposition of force to quell a disturbance. Enforcing a total curfew, like the one imposed in Milwaukee in the summer of 1967, was an example of effective use of the National Guard. In New York City, the use of the National Guard during a postal strike was effective, but its use during a sanitation strike would almost certainly have failed due to its inexperience.

Many law enforcement professionals believe that the control of riots is not a legitimate function of police, since these disturbances are too sweeping to be checked by a local police department. This belief is a dangerous abdication of responsibility. Too often in the 1960's, a mayor requested the National Guard, imposed the harshest strictures on the public, and allowed a local disturbance to escalate into a major riot. Although a mayor has the authority to call the National Guard, he seldom assumes responsibility for the use of its power in quelling a major riot. The National Guard is an army of civilians who are not qualified to deal with the complex forces at work during an incipient disturbance.

The Guard can be brutal and inexperienced, and the use of it has repeatedly demonstrated that it provokes a counter-force. As we have learned in Watts, at Attica, and at Kent State University, pitting the National Guard against people, results in local civil wars between American citizens.

The police should come to recognize that potential riots and terrorism are the greatest contemporary challenges to the efficacy of their administration and the effectiveness of their force. Every riot has had its origins in an incident between police and people that galvanized a ghetto community into action. From a police point of view, these incidents may or may not have justified the reaction of the ghetto, but the community was convinced, in virtually *every* case, that the police had acted arbitrarily, unfairly, and high handedly. Each incident could have been recognized by an intelligence agent as a potential danger. Steps should have been taken by police to counteract those people and groups who would, and did, give incendiary accounts of these incidents to inflame people into action. If a fifteen year old felon is shot in legitimate self-defense by a patrol officer, if a prisoner inadvertently dies or commits suicide while in custody, if demonstrators are legitimately arrested for breaking the law, the police must, in addition to other steps taken in each case, be sensitive to the community's reaction and particularly to those community elements who will use each case to attack the police and the social system they defend. For each incident, police should be sensitive enough to the community to issue immediately an honest, factual account of what occurred.

The police should have community relations personnel distributing and circulating factual accounts of community incidents, including material uncomplimentary to police. Admission of possible police guilt, coupled with the promise of an objective investigation and a record of impartiality, will often neutralize street rumors.

In 1967, the New York City Police Department announced that the two people killed during the East Harlem disturbances of July 23 to July 26 had been shot by policemen. The patrol officers were identified, and the case was submitted to the Grand Jury. The Department's candor did much to dispel community resentment. The police had conducted a thorough investigation and issued the findings without attempting to omit evidence or temporize. Although the police findings unquestionably subjected the city to a law suit, it is the obvious disregard of the suit's consequences that makes the police's full disclosures of the incident so commendable. A full disclosure also helps to stimulate the public's faith in the veracity and integrity of their officials.

The police should demonstrate that conspiracy will not go unpunished. The solution of the crimes planned by the Revolutionary Action Movement, and other subversive groups, tends to act as a powerful deterrent to conspiracy. Nothing is more unnerving to conspirators than a successful infiltration of their group.

The police should be at home in any area of their environment. They cannot abandon a filthy, squalid ghetto to revolutionaries who are only too content to function in isolation there. While the police must penetrate into the poor urban environment, they should also be comfortable, as they were not, in the world of middle class, college "revolutionaries" and in the upper class milieus of the Hearst and Bronfman families.

The police should recognize that effective intelligence is the indispensible ingredient of an effective riot control program. A study of the accounts of riots in Watts, Detroit, Milwaukee, Newark, Philadelphia and other cities indicates that very little intelligence was produced by investigative units as to what was really about to happen in riot areas. Local police accounts do not mention arrests for conspiracy to riot, confiscation of subversive literature, or identification of groups operating before or during riots. Yet, despite a lack of police information, newspaper reporters like Louis Lomax in Newark, readily demonstrated the existence of exploitative elements working to extend disorder. Arrests made were principally for looting, assault, disorderly conduct, and other crimes occurring during a riot. These street arrests testify to a rudimentary level of intelligence which placed the burden of law enforcement almost entirely upon the uniformed patrol officers at the riot. Police were consequently dealing with effects without much previous regard to causes.

During the Harlem riot of 1964, police actions included arrests for conspiracy to riot, the confiscation of arms, the securing of an injunction barring a revolutionary group from demonstrating, an arrest for anarchy, the taping, in a Harlem church, of an inflamatory speech calling for "guerrilla warfare," arrests of people for attempting to lead a march on a police station, the confiscation of literature on the preparation of Molotov cocktails, and the identification of the authors of that literature, These actions attested to the continuous and effective collection of intelligence by Special Services and the aggressive use by the police of that information. Pressure on actual conspirators was maintained and undoubtedly convinced many potential plotters of the unprofitability of rioting.(9)

The East Harlem disturbances of July 1967 again demonstrated the alertness of BOSSI. This incipient revolt was stopped by a combination of factors. Intelligence kept police administrators informed of all developments and plans and identified the inciters to arresting officers. Community relations officers maintained communication between the police and the people of Harlem. The Police Department saturated the area with large numbers of uniformed police who had extensive training in riot tactics. All Spanish-speaking members of the Department were assigned to work temporarily in the area. The Department prepared, and circulated to assigned police, instructional pamphlets. A high ratio of superiors to subordinates was used in the target area. Intelligence, community relations, and saturation were, however, the keys to the control of the disturbance.

The operation in Harlem was not, however, a complete

success. A great deal of undisciplined shooting by police, who thought that it would cow resisters into docility, did result in two questionable killings. A result of these killings was the issuance, in 1972, of an order that severely restricted the circumstances under which police may fire weapons.

An article in a New York City newspaper summarized the problem of riot control as involving stepped-up intelligence gathering to detect the seeds of a riot, detailed planning for coping with an outbreak, and the staging of an immediate show of force if an unruly crowd gathers.(10) The article, which reported the 1967 annual conference of the International Association of Chiefs of Police, quoted the Chief Inspector of the Philadelphia Police Department, Harry G. Fox, as stating, "Civil disorder is the number one police problem today. Good intelligence in this field is urgently needed to prevent tensions and demonstrations from maturing into fires, sniping, looting, destruction, and death."

The general awareness of police to the need of effective intelligence is steadily rising. Police departments with advanced intelligence operations should make available their expertise to other localities, and literature on police intelligence should be developed. Secrecy has served only to restrict the spread of material on intelligence; advanced, effective intelligence units should be prepared to share their expertise generously.

In the McCone Report on the Watts riot, a paragraph on the possibility of agitation and subversion during the August 1965 disorders noted:

> This is not to say that there was no agitation or promotion of the rioting by local groups or gangs which exist in pockets throughout the south central area. The sudden appearance of Molotov cocktails in quantity and the unexplained movement of men in cars through the areas of great destruction support the conclusion that there was organization and planning after the riots com-

menced. In addition, on that tense Thursday, (August 12, 1965, the day the riots began), inflammatory handbills suddenly appeared in Watts. But this cannot be identified as a master plan by one group; rather it appears to have been the work of several gangs, with membership of young men ranging in age from 14 to 35 years. All of these activities intensified the rioting and caused it to spread with increased violence from one district to another in the curfew area.(11)

This account indicates that the Los Angeles police did not appear to have anything even remotely resembling accurate intelligence on the factors at work within the riot area. The suspicions that elements were operating to spread the rioting are repeated in every account of the Watts disturbances, yet distressingly little seems to have been known by the police. The importance of good intelligence from informative liaisons within a community should become widely appreciated by police administrators, if any effective steps are to be taken to control urban rioting and terrorism.

CHAPTER VIII

Redirections

The cataclysm of Watergate and the subsequent continuing revelations about the abusive use of intelligence have revealed that the wildest and most irresponsible criticisms of the intelligence establishment pale in comparison to the reality. A President bugged his own office and then withheld his electronic evidence from Congress. A Vice President resigned when accused of accepting money illegally. During the summer and fall of 1975 it was learned that the CIA made several attempts to kill the Premier of Cuba and that a permanent unit called the "Executive Action Group" was established to plan political murders of other national leaders. The CIA, the FBI, and the National Security Agency had been wiretapping or intercepting mail. People whose political views were not liked by the administration had been harassed with frequent income tax audits. Anonymous threats, letters and forgeries became the frequently used tools of the FBI in counter-intelligence operations, most notably against Martin Luther King, Jr. Executives of federal intelligence agencies had apparently lied to Congress about the functions of their organizations. Finally, the Committee to Reelect the President, headed by a former Attorney General who had access to intelligence, used that intelligence to discredit and embarrass opponents in the primary and general elections. The American government had not only regularly employed the most reprehensible and undemocratic tactics in pursuing national policy but also had criminally tampered with the elective process.

Perhaps the most remarkable revelations concerning national intelligence operations was the publication of the Report of the U.S. Senate Select Committee on Intelligence(1), headed by Senator Frank Church. The report implicated the CIA in a number of plots to assassinate foreign leaders and indicated that the FBI under J. Edgar Hoover had threatened and harassed Martin Luther King, Jr. during the last years of his life. It seems likely that the report will reopen the investigations of King's assassination as well as the death of John F. Kennedy. The principal reform now almost certain to emerge from the intelligence investigations is a permanent Congressional oversight committee. The powers of the committee, especially to subpoena witnesses and documents are yet to be designated, but the extent of those powers will largely determine how effective the committee will be.

Meanwhile in New York City, three bills concerned with intelligence activities were considered by the City Council. They will likely be examined by the Church Committee before it makes its recommendations for national policy on intelligence gathering.

Intro. No. 780 proposed that any city agency with records on individuals not having to do with actual criminal investigations, notify that individual of the existence of such a record; not disclose that information, without the individual's permission, to anyone except another governmental agency (and require notice of such disclosure); keep a record of all inspections of the archive; permit the individual to inspect his or her own record and make copies of it; allow the individual to add anything pertinent to the record. Only the "Mayor alone" could suspend the requirements of the law concerning a specific record. The Mayor's suspension must be noted, and the individual must be notified of the suspension.

This bill was quickly followed by Intro. No. 781, which forbade the police to use "any form of electronic or photographic surveillance for identification or intelligence purposes in a matter not under actual criminal investigation except upon court order..." The court order was to be subjected to the same restrictions as a wiretap order.

Application for a wiretapping order must be made by a District Attorney or Attorney General to a justice of the Supreme Court in New York State. The target must be someone who has committed, or is about to commit, a specific crime. The application must assure that specified conversation will be recorded and that normal investigative techniques will not produce the information to be obtained through wiretapping. The identification of the telephone to be tapped must be given.

The limit of an order to wiretap, although renewable on cause, is thirty days. Results of the tap must be reported to the court, and they should match the rationale behind the original request. If they do not, an explanation is required.

Any previous applications to wiretap the target must be described, and the current application must be based on the applicant's personal knowledge. The judge may examine the applicant under oath. The applying agency must be identified, and it must minimize the possibility of recording non-critical conversations. Authorization must be obtained to enter a target's premises to install and to remove the tap. As conversations are being recorded, the justice may require progress reports at intervals he designates. An individual must be informed within ninety days of the existence of a warrant to wiretap, the period involved, and whether communications were intercepted. The justice may release portions of the recorded material to the target.

Any knowledge obtained by wiretapping may be used in court if it relates to the warrant. If the information is criminal, but outside the scope described in the order, the judge's permission to amend the warrant must be sought before the information can be used. A target must be given at least ten days notice before the evidence obtained from a tap can be used in a trial against him. The judge must report to the U.S. Court the results of the tap within thirty days, to comply with federal law. His report insures federal monitoring of the process and extends judicial accountability, especially in cases involving organized crime. Wiretapping has been used effectively against organized crime, but the controls, like the disclosure rule and the narrow definitions in this bill, may seem excessively restrictive to general intelligence agencies, because police agents have in the past abused the law to tap and penetrate the ranks of organized crime.

Intro. No. 782 requires a court order to "place police agents undercover in groups or organizations." The court order would be governed by the same restrictions that are placed on wiretap orders.

These three proposals provide examples of the kind of ill-advised legislation that may become law as a reaction to the national abuses of intelligence that Watergate and the Church Committee have uncovered. Although these abuses have not been discovered on a local level, it may be informative to national legislators to measure the City Council proposals against the history and activities of BOSSI when that unit was operating effectively and legally as an investigative agency.

BOSSI was established to investigate aliens who had entered the country illegally. Its work focused on the alien and the foreign-born, whether they were communists and anarchists in the 1930's or were German and Japanese during World War II. The transition from investigating aliens to investigating Americans who were sympathetic to "alien" or "foreign" causes and philosophies occurred gradually and almost imperceptibly. Labor leaders were suspected of being communist because they wanted rights for workers, and Americans suggesting social reforms were thought to be socialists. During the 1960's, the Vietnam War polarized people's convictions, and those who opposed the war were thought by intelligence units to be supporting the communist Viet Cong government and were therefore "alien" and "subversive." When Martin Luther King, Jr. called for the end of hostilities in Vietnam, many considered him as "un-American" as the students at Kent State who were protesting the war. They were "aliens," and given the generally politically right orientation of the police establishment, they were subversives, subject to surveillance. When young National Guard citizens opened fire and killed American students at Kent State, a civil war had begun. Intelligence had turned Americans against Americans, and everyone seemed to be an "alien." Investigative agencies had, without any monitoring control from the elected officials of the American people, extended their intelligence work against the people themselves. Even a national leader like Martin Luther King was not exempt from FBI surveillance and harassment. As the Church committee has indicated some kind of criteria is needed to control and monitor investigative agencies and protect individual privacy.

However, as I have tried to stress in this book, the need for intelligence-gathering remains, because assassination attempts against a President and candidates continue to occur, union strife will intensify as unemployment and inflation continue, and terrorism becomes a frequently used public act. One federal intelligence official (2) indicated that twenty persons had been killed and a hundred and twenty-two people had been injured by bombs in the United States from May 1, 1974 to April 30, 1975. During the first nine months of 1975, bombs killed forty-two people and injured two hundred and forty-two others. Another report (3) cited 2,041 bombing attacks during 1974. Finally, Brook McClure (4) summarized recommendations for continued intelligence by stating:

> One of the most serious problems in connection with terrorism is inadequate police intelligence capacity. The techniques of police intelligence— penetration of suspicious groups, dossier-keeping, cultivation of informers, undercover activities in general—disturb the average citizen. Yet the problem of terrorism is essentially one of counterintelligence—of frustrating and neutralizing plans and breaking up secret conspiracies by small groups of people seeking to destroy the

state. The penalty of failure is death to innocent people, destruction of property, and intimidation of the public in a continuous upward spiral.

If needed intelligence-gathering is to continue, the three proposals of the City Council in New York City would certainly provide for the protection of privacy but would seriously hamper police intelligence and endanger the public's safety. Information in intelligence files would be greatly reduced. To inform a target of surveillance would nullify and invalidate much of the data that might be collected. Tracking beepers could not be used in kidnapping cases. Events could not be monitored until they had become violent, and closed circuit television cameras could not be used to assess demonstrations.

An undercover agent gains legitimacy and acceptance by drifting in and out of groups that permit evaluation of their intent. Ultimately, the criminal purposes of a group become obvious. The Statue of Liberty plot could not have been intercepted without Ray Wood's participation in many activities, including those of the Congress of Racial Equality with whom he gained visibility and acceptance. The Intro proposals would not allow Wood to move among groups as he did.

On August 26, 1968, William Hoff, a longtime sympathizer with right wing organizations was arrested after he gave an undercover operator two cans of explosives with instructions to place them in the doorways of two liberals' residences. The arrest was the result of having an undercover agent investigate the activities of militant right wing individuals in New York City. The arrest netted a list of four or five typewritten pages of potential targets found on Hoff. The investigation was initiated before Hoff had engaged in any criminal activity and was done for general intelligence-gathering. Under the Intro proposals, it is highly unlikely that judicial authority would approve of this kind of investigation which, had it not been made, would have allowed an undetected Hoff to kill people and damage property.

In April of 1968, Detectives Wayne Carrington and

Timothy L. Hubbard were undercover police officers assigned to attend an anti-Vietnam War conference at the Diplomat Hotel in New York City. At the conference, they met a group whose confidence they gained after attending many subsequent rallies. Carrington and Hubbard learned that the group was planning to burglarize an armory to obtain arms for the ultimate goal of "killing a cop a week." The individuals were arrested before their robbery was attempted. Four of six people were convicted of possession of bombs and firearms. The investigation and arrests were made possible only after BOSSI had assigned the agents to the conference and had ordered them to maintain friendships with any individuals they met. Under the Intro bills, the assignment to the conference would have been improper. Without police interference, the individuals plotting to kill police officers might well have been successful in carrying out their conspiracy.

I have described BOSSI's infiltration into the Black Panther Party elsewhere. It must be remembered that although they were alleged to conduct political educational classes, para-military training, street demonstrations, and free food programs, the publicly available literature of the Panthers used revolutionary rhetoric and advocated the acquisition and use to firearms to "defend" black rights. With this information, BOSSI assigned police officers to infiltrate the Black Panther Party.

A significant discovery of the investigation of the Panthers was made by Ralph White who in January of 1969, found the hiding place of twenty-four sticks of dynamite. White was directed by BOSSI to take the case of dynamite to the Bomb Squad where the explosives were replaced by an inert substance. White returned the case to its original location. These sticks were later found to have been mixed with other sticks of dynamite and placed by Panthers at the 24th and 44th Precinct station houses. The resulting explosions were of minimal size due to the substitution of inert material for dynamite in some of the sticks.

BOSSI's investigative work revealed much about the nature and workings of the Black Panther Party. Many of the Panthers observed later became members of the Black Liberation Army and engaged in armed robberies across the country, killing and wounding many police officers. Although this investigation was initiated on the basis of the rhetoric and publicly stated goals of the Black Panther Party, such surveillance of another group today would not be possible under the Intro proposals.

In 1970, Detective Steve Weiner as an undercover agent maintaining contacts with known "new left" radicals and appearing to be a radical himself, was approached by Robin Palmer to join a criminal conspiracy. As a result, Palmer and five others were arrested and convicted on charges of attempting to firebomb the First National City Bank at Madison Avenue and East 91st Street in New York. Prior to being asked to join the conspiracy by Palmer, Detective Weiner, under proposed guidelines, would have no authorization to maintain the vague and informative contacts he had established.

BOSSI assigned many undercover agents to gather intelligence on the large and frequently disorderly and disruptive demonstrations held to protest the Vietnam War. At least one agent knew Sam Melville, Jane Alpert, and other young radicals when they were making and planting bombs in New York City. On June 20, 1967, eighteen indictments were made by a Queens County Grand Jury for various criminal charges including conspiracy to commit arson, anarchy, possession of dangerous weapons, and conspiracy to commit homicide. Herman Ferguson, an assistant principal in the city school system, and Arthur Harris, were found guilty of conspiring to kill Whitney Young of the Urban League and Roy Wilkins of the National Association for the Advancement of Colored People. Both Ferguson and Harris disappeared after being freed on bail.

Other individuals, arrested on June 21, 1967, were not involved with homicide, but did conspire to set fire to gasoline stations, lumber yards and subway stations. In plotting to overthrow the government, they practiced with rifles and pistols at various ranges. These people either pleaded guilty or were found guilty of possession of dangerous weapons. All of these people were members of, or active in, the Revolutionary Action Movement and/or the Jamaica Rifle and Pistol Club, a front organization for the Movement.

The detectives responsible for bringing these people to trial were undercover agents Edward Howlette and Abraham Duncan. Howlette met the plotters when he was assigned to investigate the organizing of demonstrations to protest the mural, "Banjo Billy," painted on the wall of the Jamaica Savings Bank in Queens. He was later included in other plans of the group, including "political education" classes, firearm practice, and discussions and preparations to kill Young and Wilkins. Detective Duncan became involved with the investigation when he began to attend classes in the Black Repertory Theatre and School headed by Leroi Jones.

It is impossible either to estimate or ignore the impact of the operations of would-be plotters against the public as well as against a union leader, a visiting dignitary or a President. It is at least minimally reasonable to expect that potential assassins, kidnappers, and terrorists be inhibited by the knowledge that intelligence units can be effective. Yet few of the conspiracies that BOSSI infiltrated and interrupted could have been stopped without the use of proactive intelligence techniques that are curtailed in the City Council legislation.

How to redirect and redistribute the power of intelligence is not a simple matter. Should the power of police department executives be extended or decreased? When I think about the history of BOSSI during the 1960's, I am reminded of the bleak day when Malcolm X was killed. We knew that the potentiality of a killing existed, and we warned Malcolm of the danger and suggested bodyguards. The black leader refused protection and lost his life because of it. Should the police department have insisted on protection against Malcolm's rights of privacy?

A partial answer to that question seems to be indicated in the legislative intent in New York State's Freedom of Information Law. This law serves as an eloquent guide to redistributing the power of police intelligence to those like Malcolm who are threatened and those who are under general investigation:

> The legislature hereby finds that a free society is maintained when government is responsive and responsible to the public, and when the public is aware of government actions. The more open a government is with its citizenry, the greater the understanding and participation of the public in government.
>
> As state and local government services increase and public problems become more sophisticated and complex and therefore harder to solve, and with the resultant increase in revenues and expenditures, it is incumbent on the state and its localities to extend public accountability wherever and whenever feasible.
>
> The people's right to know the process of government decision-making and the documents and statistics leading to determinations is basic to our society. Access to such information should not be thwarted by shrouding it with the cloak of secrecy or confidentiality.
>
> The legislature therefore declares that government is the public's business and that the public, individually and collectively and represented by a free news media, should have unimpaired access to the records.

The Freedom of Information Law opens the processes of government to public scrutiny by making all kinds of records and documents available for inspection. It is a reasonable act, for it insures the accountability of the government, and of the criminal justice system to the people they serve.

That a redirection of intelligence activities is needed is apparent from the Church Committee's report and the revelations of the Watergate hearings. Instead of adopting the overreactive measures of the Intro proposals, legislators might very well consider a monitoring, oversight authority over intelligence-gathering that would be representative, not repressive, of the constitutional rights of American citizens. That authority might be governed by the consumerism that has been reflected in other citizens' groups. Americans elect and pay their representatives to maintain the kind of government and intelligence operations that their taxes support. If representative government works, then a monitoring authority with legal power to exact accountability from intelligence agencies should represent the public consumer-citizens by providing access to government records and should legally protect public safety. In a democracy, people have a right, if not an obligation, to know what their government and their criminal justice system does and to hold their elected representatives, as monitors, accountable.

People, as citizens with the right to learn what information their government possesses about them and as voter-consumers with the right to change their representatives and government at the polls, must be the final "unit" of surveillance in a democracy. A monitoring oversight committee, with limited or extensive legal powers, is as susceptible to abuses as those whom they monitor. Investigation committees monitoring investigative agencies again threatens Big Brother government. As we learn and forget almost daily, citizens in a democracy, if they are actively concerned with their government and their well-being, determine what their government is and is not. As voters, consumers, and citizens with democratic representation, they must decide what under law intelligence should or should not be.

Notes

CHAPTER II. MANDATE AND HISTORY

(1) *New York City Charter,* Section 435. Albany: William Press, 1943.

(2) *The World Almanac and Book of Facts.* New York: New York *World Telegram and Sun,* 1966.

(3) *Municipal Police Administration.* Chicago: The International City Manager's Association, 1954, p.456.

(4) United States Congress, Senate, Commission on Organization of the Executive Branch of the Government, (Hoover Commission). *Task Force Report on Intelligence Activities.* Washington: U.S. Government Printing Office, 1955.

(5) O.W. Wilson, *Police Administration.* New York: McGraw-Hill, 1950 and 1963, p.119.

(6) *A Survey of the Police Department –Baltimore, Maryland.* Washington: The International Association of Chiefs of Police, December 1965.

(7) Wilson, *op. cit.,* Revised 1963, pp. 119-20.

(8) Don Whitehead, *The F.B.I. Story.* New York: Random House, foreword.

(9) *The President's Commission on the Assassination of President John F. Kennedy.* (The Warren Report). Washington, D.C., Government Printing Office, 1964,p.186.

(10) Mark Sherwin, *The Extremists.* New York: St. Martin's Press, 1963, Introduction.

(11) *Violence in the City–An End or a Beginning? A Report by the Governor's Commission on the Los Angeles Riots,* Dec. 2, 1965.

(12) *President's Commission on the Assassination . . .op. cit.* 1964, p. 196.

CHAPTER III. ADMINISTRATION AND PERSONNEL

(1) Chief Thomas J. Cahill, "Intelligence Unit is a Key Division of a Police Agency," *FBI Law Enforcement Bulletin* Vol. 31, No.9, September, 1962, p. 15.

(2) For detailed treatment of this subject see David Wise & Thomas B. Ross's, *The Invisible Government,* New York: Random House, 1964, p. 190.

(3) W. Cleon Skousen, "The Intelligence Unit," *Law and Order,* Vol. 14, No. 6, June, 1966, p. 68.

(4) Chief Inspector Francis J. M. Robb commanded the Unit in 1953 and 1954, Chief Inspector, Sanford D. Garelik, was in command from 1960 to 1962.

(5) O.W. Wilson, *Police Administration.* New York: McGraw-Hill, 1950 and 1963, p. 120

(6) These cases receive more detailed discussion later in this book.

(7) "American Communism," edited by Acting Captain George A. Gallagher, Special Squad #1, Police Department, New York City, 1944; the library of the Bureau of Special Services.

(8) The President's Commission on Law Enforcement and the Administration of Justice, *Task Force Report: The Police,* 1967, p. 126.

(9) Andrew Tully, *CIA: The Inside Story.* New York: William Morrow, 1962, p. 25.

(10) Skousen, *op. cit.,* June 1966, p. 68.

(11) *Municipal Police Administration.* Chicago: The International City Manager's Association, 1950, p. 93.

(12) Allen Dulles, *The Craft of Intelligence.* New York: Harper and Row, 1965, p. 168.

(13) Allen Dulles. *op. cit.* 1965, p. 81.

(14) Andrew Tully, *op. cit.,* 1962, p. 25.

(15) Wise and Ross, *op. cit.,* p. 224.

CHAPTER IV. SUBVERSION

(1) Addison H. Fording, "Policing a Student Revolt." *Police,* November-December 1966, p. 71

(2) W. Cleon Skousen, *"The Intelligence Unit".* *Law and Order,* Vol. 14, No. 6, June 1966, p. 68.

(3) For further details on these and related cases see Allen Dulles, *The Craft of Intelligence.* New York: The New American Library, 1963, pp. 100-110.

(4) Skousen, *op. cit.,* June 1966, p. 68.

(5) Inspector George P. McManus, New York City Police Department, "Practical Measures for Police Control of Riots and Mobs." *FBI Law Enforcement Bulletin,* U.S. Department of Justice, October 1962, p.3

(6) David Wise and Thomas B. Ross, *The Invisible Government.* New York: Random House, 1964, p. 356.

(7) Thomas J. McGreevy wrote on these subjects in an article titled "Police Intelligence Operations". *Police,* March-April 1964 p. 46.

(8) For more detailed treatment of this material, see Andrew Tully, *CIA: The Inside Story.* New York: William Morrow, 1962.

(9) New York District Attorney Frank Hogan testimony before the Senate Judiciary Subcommittee on July 12, 1967 in Washington, D.C. This view was supported by a spokesman for the New York District Attorneys Association and the National District Attorneys Association testifying before the same Subcommittee on April 20, 1967.

(10) This material and the following data on the organization's objectives were taken from a Minutemen publication entitled "A Short History of the Minutemen." This is a pamphlet distributed by the Minutemen organization and quoted at length in a report submitted by the Attorney General of California, Thomas C. Lynch, to State Senator J. Eugene McAteer of California on April 12, 1965.

(11) The New York *Times* and the now defunct *World-Journal-Tribune* newspapers carried comprehensive accounts of these arrests in the November 1, 2 and 3, 1966 issues.

(12) This plot received detailed coverage in the press, especially New York *Daily News* of June 22, 1967 and The New York *Times* of the same date. *Sepia Publication* of 1220 Harding St., Fort Worth, Texas carried a lengthy article in its September 1967 issue entitled "The Strange Plot to Kill Roy Wilkins."

(13) This and other accounts on this case were reported in The New York *Times* during the arrests in February 1965 and the subsequent trial in May 1965.

(14) A penetrating insight into the workings of this organization was furnished by Philip Luce, a disaffected member of the group, writing in the May 8, 1965 *Saturday Evening Post* in an article entitled "Why I Quit the Extreme Left."

(15) The New York *Times,* August 3, 1975.

(16) The Newark riot is discussed later in this chapter.

(17) See the New York *Times* issues of late July and August, 1964 for details on the legal battles involving Progressive Labor Movement and their involvement in the riots.

(18) The New York *Herald Tribune* February 23, 1965. This account includes reports on the police offer of protection for Malcolm as well as a general description of the functions of the Bureau of Special Services.

(19) The definitive work on the Nation of Islam, its origins, history and direction is C. Eric Lincoln, *The Black Muslims in America*. Boston: Beacon Press, 1961.

(20) *Ibid* p. 5, 27.

(21) *A Survey of the Police Department - Baltimore, Maryland*, by the International Association of Chiefs of Police, 1319 Eighteenth St., N.W., Washington, D.C., December 1965, pp. 53, 133, 134.

(22) *An Organizational Study of the Police Department, New York City*, by the International Association of Chiefs of Police, 1319 Eighteenth St., N.W., Washington D.C., July 1967, pp. 468, 469.

(23) "The Anatomy of Black Power" by Louis E. Lomax. A series of five articles appearing in the Long Island *Press* on August 27, 28, 29, 30 and 31, 1967. Mr. Lomax has authored *The Negro Revolt* and *The Reluctant African*.

(24) Chief Thomas J. Cahill, San Francisco Police Department, "Intelligence Unit is a Key Division of a Police Agency." *F.B.I. Law Enforcement Bulletin*, September 1962, p. 15.

(25) Allen Dulles testifying before Congress in 1947. Quoted by Andrew Tully in *CIA: The Inside Story*. New York: William Morrow 1962, p. 11.

(26) David A. McCandless, "Consideration on Racial Tension." *Police*, Sept.-Oct. 1964, p. 40.

CHAPTER V. SECURITY FOR DIGNITARIES

(1) For a detailed, minute-by-minute account of this visit and an analysis of police preparations made in connection with this event see *Police Management Review*. Planning Bureau, New York City Police Department, Volume 3, numbers 3, 4, 5 and Volume 4, numbers 1 and 2: April, May, June, September, October 1966.

(2) *Universal Standard Encyclopedia*. New York: Standard Reference Works Publishing Co., 1956, Volumes X, XV, pp. 3605, 5332, 5636.

(3) Arthur M. Schlessinger Jr., *A Thousand Days*. Boston: Houghton Mifflin Co., 1965, p. 678.

(4) Alan Clark, *Barbarossa*. New York: William Morrow & Co., 1960, p. 27.

(5) It is interesting that former Secret Service Chief U.E.

Baughman noted in his book that the threat to American Presidents came almost exclusively from the mentally deranged. Mr. Baughman did not take the possibility of a conspiracy very seriously despite the fact that the celebrated attempt on President Truman by Puerto Rican Nationalists occurred during his administration. *Secret Service Chief.* NewYork: Harper & Bros. 1962, p. 37.

(6) *The President's Commission on the Assassination of President John F. Kennedy.* (The Warren Report). Washington D.C: Government Printing Office, 1964, p. 204.

(7) Lawrence Zelio Freedman, "Profile of an Assassin," *Police,* Vol. VII, March-April 1966, p. 26.

(8) *The President's Commission on the Assassination . . .op. cit., p. 200.*

(9) *Ibid.*, p. 196.

(10) This security breakdown is examined in greater detail in Andrew Tully, *CIA: The Inside Story.* New York: William Morrow & Company, 1962, p. 70.

(11) Remarks of Police Commissioner Michael J. Murphy at the 61st Annual Conference of the New York State Association of Chiefs of Police, Glen Falls, New York, Tuesday, July 25, 1961.

(12) *The President's Commission on the Assassination . . .op. cit.* p. 186

(13) *Ibid,* p. 185.

(14) *Standard Operating Procedure #10, Security Measures—Presidential Visits,* New York City Police Department, October 12, 1964.

CHAPTER VI. LABOR DISPUTES

(1) "American Communism", edited by Acting Captain George G. Gallagher, Special Squad #1, Police Department, New York City, 1944, in the library of the Bureau of Special Services, p. 46.

(2) Donald C. Stone, "The Public Interest In Labor Disputes," *The City's Role in Strikes.* Chicago: International City Manager's Association; 1937, pp. 5-9.

(3) For more complete treatment of the strike, the issues, the incidents and the surrounding circumstances see The New York *Times* which carried almost daily accounts of this controversy throughout its course.

(4) The Condon-Wadlin Act was succeeded by the Taylor Law, on September 1, 1967. The new law is presumed to address itself more realistically to the problem of strikes by public employees by

aiming its fire at the union and its officers while adopting a system of lighter penalties for the strikers. The first application of this law came in September 1967 when President Albert Shanker of the United Federation of Teachers Union received a five day jail sentence and the union was fined for striking the New York City school system.

(5) *Rules and Procedures of the New York City Police Department,* November 1, 1963, Chapter 16, p. 179.

(6) The principles enumerated in the foregoing decisions can be found in the following cases, among others; *Stillwell Theatre Inc. v. Kaplan,* 259 N.Y. 405; *People v. Ward,* 272, N.Y. 615; *Goldfinger v. Feintuch,* 276, N.Y. 218; *Supreme Court decision* re: *Transport Workers Union; U.S. Supreme Court, N.Y. Alliance v. Sanitary Grocery Co; Milgram's case,* also *People v. Jenkins,* 138, Misc. 498; *People v. Hopkins,* 147 Misc. 12; *People v. Kayl,* 165, Misc. 663.

(7) Timothy J. Walsh, *"Law Enforcement Control In Labor Disturbances." Police,* Vol. 8 no. 6, July-August 1964, p. 25.

(8) *Ibid,* 1964.

(9) *Ibid,* p. 26.

CHAPTER VII. LIAISONS AND POLICY

(1) Attorney General Arthur J. Sills addressing the Metropolitan Regional Council on January 30, 1964. Teaneck, New Jersey.

(2) *The President's Commission on the Assassination of President John F. Kennedy* (The Warren Report). Washington, D.C.: Government Printing Office, 1964, p.13.

(3) United States Department of Justice, *F.B.I. Annual Report, Fiscal Year* 1965, 1966, p. 23.

(4) United States, The President's Commission on Law Enforcement, and Administration of Justice, *Task Force Report: The Police,* 1967, p. 80.

(5) Harry W. More Jr., "Federal Personnel Loyalty—Security Programs." *Police,* Vol. 8 no. 4, March-April 1964, p. 20.

(6) United States Congress, House, Committee on Un-American Activities, *Guide to Subversive Organizations and Publications,* 87th Congress, 2d Session, 1961, p. 18.

(7) The New York *Times* carried accounts of these disclosures in its editions of October 1st through October 15, 1967.

(8) *An Organizational Study of the Police Department, New York City, New York,* by the International Association of Chiefs of Police 1319 Eighteenth St., N.W., Washington, D.C., July 1967, pp 468-470

(9) See the request for a temporary injunction submitted by the New York City Corporation Counsel to Judge Gerald P. Culkin of the New York State Supreme Court on August 4, 1964. Order granted same day. For further details on arrests, police activity and resume of events see The New York *Times* from July 25, 1964 to August 10, 1964.

(10) The New York *Post*, September 14, 1967

(11) *Violence in the City–An End or a Beginning?* A Report by the Governor's Commission on the Los Angeles Riots, December 2, 1965.

CHAPTER VIII. REDIRECTIONS

(1) U.S. Senate Select Committee on Intelligence, *Alleged Assasination Plots Involving Foreign Leaders*. Washington, D.C.: Government Printing Office, Senate Report 94-465, 1975.

(2) Brooks McClure, Special Assistant, Directorate of International Security Affairs, Department of Defense.

(3) Report of the Senate International Security Subcommittee.

(4) Brooks McClure.

Bibliography

ARTICLES AND PERIODICALS

Cahill, Thomas J. Chief, San Francisco Police Department "Intelligence Unit in a Key Division of a Police Agency." *F.B.I. Law Enforcement Bulletin,* September 1962.

F.B.I. Law Enforcement Bulletin. Washington, D.C. 1960-75.

Fording, Addison H. "Policing A Student Revolt." *Police Magazine,* November-December 1966.

Law and Order Magazine. New York, Copp Publications, Inc. 1965-67.

Law Enforcement Executive. Office for Local Government. State of New York. February 1967.

Lomax, Louis. "The Anatomy of Black Power." *Long Island Press,* August 27-31, 1967.

Luce, Philip. "Why I Quit the Extreme Left." *Saturday Evening Post, May 8, 1965.*

McCandless, David A. "Consideration of Racial Tension." *Police Magazine,* September-October 1964.

McGreevy, Thomas J. "Police Intelligence Operations." *Police Magazine,* March-April 1964.

McManus, George P. Inspector New York City Police Department. "Practical Measures for Police Control of Riots and Mobs." *F.B.I. Law Enforcement Bulletin,* October 1962.

Police Magazine. Springfield, Ill., Charles C. Thomas, 1960-67.

Police Management Review. Planning Bureau, New York City Police Department, 1963-67.

Police Yearbook. International Association of Chiefs of Police, Washington, D.C. 1964-66.

Skousen, W. Cleon. "The Intelligence Unit." *Law and Order Magazine,* June 1966.

Stone, Donald C. "The Public Interest in Labor Disputes." *The City's Role in Strikes.* Chicago, International City Manager's Association, 1937.

"The Strange Plot to Kill Roy Wilkins." *Sepia Publications*, September 1967.
World Almanac and Book of Facts. New York, World Telegram and Sun, 1966.

BOOKS

Alsop, Stewart and Thomas Braden. *Sub Rosa-The OSS and American Espionage*. New York, Harcourt, Brace & World, 1946.
Bassiouni, M. Cherif, (Ed.) *The Law of Dissent and Riots*. Springfield, Ill. Charles C. Thomas, 1969.
Baughman, U.E. *Secret Service Chief*. New York, Harper & Bros., 1962.
Bedau, Hugo Adam. *Civil Disobedience*. New York, Pegasus, 1969
Black, Algernon D. *The People and the Police*, New York, McGraw Hill, 1968.
Burnham, James. *The Web of Subversion*. New York, John Day Co., 1954
Cahalane, Cornelius F. *The Policeman's Guide*. New York, Harper & Bros., 1952.
Chenigny, Paul. *Cops and Rebels*. New York. Curtis Books, 1972.
Clark, Alan. *Barbarossa*. New York, William Morrow & Co., 1960.
Cook, Fred J. *The FBI Nobody Knows*. New York, Pyramid Books, 1964.
Cookridge, E.H. *Gehlen - Spy of the Century*. New York, Random House, 1971.
Daniel, Robert S. (Ed.) *Contemporary Readings in General Psychology*. Boston, Houghton Mifflin Co., 1959.
Donovan, Robert J. *The Assassins*. New York, Harper & Bros., 1952.
Dudycha, George J. *Psychology for Law Enforcement Officers*. Springfield, Ill. Charles C. Thomas, 1955.
Dulles, Allen. *The Craft of Intelligence*. New York, The New American Library, 1963.
Eckstein, Harry (Ed.) *Internal War*, New York, The Free Press. 1964.
Essien-Udom, E.U. *Black Nationalism*. New York, Dell Publishing Co., 1962.
Forman, James. *The Making of Black Revolutionaries*. New York, The Macmillan Co., 1972.
Havens, Murray Clark, Carl Leiden, and Karl M. Schmitt. *The*

Politics of Assassination, Englewood Cliffs, N.J. Prentice-Hall, Inc., 1970.

Hayden, Tom. *Rebellion and Repression*. New York, World Publishing Co., 1969.

Hoover, J. Edgar. *Masters of Deceit*. New York, Pocket Books, Inc., 1958.

Hunt, E. Howard. *Undercover*. New York, Berkeley Publishing Corp., 1974.

Jacobs, Harold (Ed.) *Weatherman*. Palo Alto, Calif., 1970.

Jones, J. Harry. *The Minutemen*. Garden City, N.Y. Doubleday & Co., 1968.

Kirkham, James F., Sheldon G. Levy, and William J. Crotty. *Assassination and Political Violence*. Washington, D.C., U.S. Government Printing Office, 1969.

Kirkpatrick, Lyman B., Jr. *The United States Intelligence Community*. New York, Hill and Wang, 1973.

Leonard, V.A. *Police Organization and Management*. Brooklyn, New York, The Foundation Press, Inc., 1951.

Lincoln, C. Eric. *The Black Muslims in America*. Boston, Beacon Press, 1961.

Mac Iver, Robert M. *The Web of Government*. New York, The Macmillan Co., 1965.

Marchetti, Victor and John D. Marks. *The CIA and the Cult of Intelligence*. New York, Alfred A. Knopf, 1974.

Masotti, Louis H. and Don R. Bowen (Eds.) *Riots and Rebellion: Civil Violence in the Urban Community*. Beverly Hills, Calif., Sage Publications, Inc., 1968.

Methvin, Eugene H. *The Riot Makers*. New Rochelle, N.Y. Arlington House, 1970.

Momboisse, Raymond M. *Blueprint of Revolution*. Springfield, Ill., Charles C. Thomas, 1970.

Municipal Police Administration, International City Manager's Association, Chicago, Ill., 1954.

Municipal Police Personnel Administration, International City Manager's Association, Chicago, Ill., 1950.

Nelson, Truman. *The Torture of Mothers*. Newberry Post, Mass., The Garrison Press, 1964.

Nieburg, Harold L. *Political Violence: The Behavioral Process*, New York, St. Martin's Press, 1969.

Overstreet, Harry and Bonaro Overstreet *The FBI in Our Open Society*. New York, W.W. Norton & Co., 1969.

Penkovskiy, Olez *The Penkovskiy Papers*. Garden City, N.Y., Doubleday & Co., 1965.

Pinto, Oreste. *Spy Catcher*. New York, Berkeley Publishing Corp., 1952.

Ransom, Harry Howe. *Central Intelligence and National Security*. Cambridge, Mass., Harvard University Press, 1958.

Ransom, Harry Howe. *The Intelligence Establishment*. Cambridge, Mass., Harvard University Press, 1970.

Reitman, Alan. *The Price of Liberty*. New York, W.W. Norton & Co., 1968.

Rosenberg, Jerry M. *The Death of Privacy*. New York, Random House, 1969.

Rowan, Richard Wilmer *The Story of Secret Service*. Garden City, New York, Doubleday, 1937.

Rule, James B. *Private Lives and Public Surveillance*. New York, Schocken Books, 1974.

Sayre, Wallace S. and Herbert Kaufman. *Governing New York City*. New York, W.W. Norton & Co., 1965.

Schlessinger, Arthur M. *A Thousand Days*. Boston, Houghton Mifflin Co., 1965.

Schultz, Donald O. *Police Operational Intelligence*. Springfield, Ill., Charles C. Thomas, 1968.

Sherman, Lawrence W. (Ed.) *Police Corruption*. Garden City, New York, Anchor Books, 1974.

Sherwin, Mark. *The Extremists*. New York, St. Martin's Press.

Stahl, Sussmann and Neil J. Bloomfield (Eds.) *The Community and Racial Crises*. New York, Practising Law Institute, 1966.

Tully, Andrew. *CIA: The Inside Story*. New York, William Morrow & Co., 1962.

Tully, Andrew. *The FBI's Most Famous Cases*. New York, Dell Publishing Co., 1965.

Tully, Andrew. *The Super Spies*. New York, William Morrow & Co., 1969.

Turner, William W. *Hoover's FBI*. Los Angeles, Sherbourne Press, 1970.

Universal Standard Encyclopedia. New York, Standard Reference Works Publishing Co., 1956.

Veysey, Laurence (Ed.) *Law and Resistance: American Attitudes toward Authority*. New York, Harper & Row, 1970.

Westin, Alan F. *Privacy and Freedom*. New York, Atheneum, 1967.

Westley, William A. *Violence and the Police*. Cambridge, Mass., MIT Press, 1970.

White, Theodore H. *The Making of the President*, 1964. New York, Atheneum, 1965.

Whitehead, Donald. The FBI Story: A Report to the People. New York, Random House, 1956.

Wilson, O.W. *Police Administration.* New York, McGraw-Hill Book Co., 1963.

Wise, David and Thomas B. Ross. *The Invisible Government.* New York, Random House, 1964.

Youngblood, Rufus W. *Twenty Years in the Secret Service.* New York, Simon & Schuster, 1973.

Zinn, Howard. *Disobedience and Democracy.* New York, Vintage Books, 1968.

REPORTS

Challenge of Crime in a Free Society. A Report by the President's Commission on Law Enforcement and the Administration of Justice, Washington, D.C., U.S. Government Printing Office, February, 1967.

Commission to Investigate Allegations of Police Corruption and the City's Anti-corruption Procedures. New York, Bar Press, 1972.

The Computer and Invasion of Privacy. New York, Arno Press, 1967.

Crisis at Columbia: Report of the Fact Finding Commission Appointed to Investigate the Disturbances at Columbia University, April and May, 1968. New York, Vintage Books, 1968.

FBI Annual Report. Washington, D.C., U.S. Department of Justice, Fiscal Year, 1965.

Malcolm X Speaks. New York, Merit Publishers, 1965.

An Organizational Study of the Police Department, New York City, New York. International Association of Chiefs of Police, Washington, D.C., 1967.

Para-Military Organizations in California. Department of Justice, State of California, 1965.

Report of the National Advisory Commission on Civil Disorders. Washington, D.C., U.S. Government Printing Office, 1968.

The Report of the President's Commission of Campus Unrest, New York, Arno Press, 1970.

Surveillance, Dataveillance and Personal Freedoms. Fairlawn, New Jersey, R.E. Burdick, Inc., 1972.

Survey of the Police Department, Baltimore, Maryland. International Association of Chiefs of Police, 1965.

Task Force Report: The Police. The President's Commission on Law Enforcement and the Administration of Justice, 1967.

Violence in the City: An End or a Beginning? A Report by the Governor's Commission on the Los Angeles Riots, 1965.

Warren Report: A Report of the President's Commission on the

Assassination of President John F. Kennedy. New York, The Associated Press, 1964.

UNPUBLISHED MATERIAL

Gallagher, George G. Acting Captain, New York City Police Department (ed.) *American Communism* 1944.

NEWSPAPERS

Herald Tribune. 1964-66.
New York Daily News. 1965-75.
New York Post. 1964-67.
New York Times. 1960-75.
World-Journal Telegram. 1966-67.

PUBLIC DOCUMENTS

Committee on Un-American Activities, U.S. House of Representatives. Washington D.C., various publications issued by this agency.
Manual for Police in the State of New York. Albany, 1966.
New York City Charter.
Rules and Procedures of the New York City Police Department.
Standard Operating Procedures, Press Releases, other orders of the New York City Police Department.
U.S. Congress, House Committee on Un-American Activities. *Guide to Subversive Organizations and Publications*. 87th Congress, 2nd Session, 1961.
U.S. Congress, Senate, Commission on Organization of the Executive Branch of the Government, (Hoover Commission). *Task Force Report on Intelligence Activities*. Washington, U.S. Government Printing Office, 1955.
U.S. Congress, Senate, An Interim Report of the Select Committee to Study Governmental Operations with Respect to Intelligence Activities (Church Committee). *Alleged Assassination Plots Involving Foreign Leaders*. Washington, D.C., U.S. Government Printing Office, 1975.
U.S. Congress, Senate, Internal Security Subcommittee reports on testimony of Brooks McClure and others, 1975.

Index

A

abuses (of intelligence), 7, 10, 50-1, 60, 94, 146, 160, 163
Administrative Vice Division, 152
aliens, 18, 24, 28, 138, 142-43, 163-64
Aguiji-Ironsi, Johnson, T.U., 99
Alpert, Jane, 167
Ameer, Leon, 85
American Committee for the Protection of the Foreign Born, 142
American Nazi Party, 4, 16, 25, 53, 94, 148
Arafat, Yassir, 102, 106-07
Armas, Carlos Castillo, 99
arrests, 4, 7, 10, 21, 32, 35, 73, 79, 90, 93, 108, 165-67
Attica State Prison, 155
assassinations, 5, 7, 51, 81, 84-91, 97-101, 109-110, 112, 114, 116-17, 119-20, 161, 164, 168
assignments, 35-37, 43, 102-08, 133

B

Balewa, Abubaker Tafewa, 99

Bandaranaike, S.W.R.D., 99
Bantam Books, Inc. v. Sullivan, 81
Batista, Fulgencio, 102
Bay of Pigs "invasion," 29, 34, 146
Birch Society, John, 16, 25
Black Liberation Army, 7, 167
Black Liberation Front, 75-81
Black Muslims, 16, 52, 84-86, 94
Black Nationalists, 16, 25, 100
Black Panthers, 4, 78, 166-67
Black Repertory Theatre and School, 168
Bomb Squad, *see:* Radical Squad, 24
Bomb Squad, 104, 114, 166
bombings, 4, 7, 8, 73-74, 76-77, 101, 164-67
Bormann, Martin, 46
Bowe, Walter, 76
Bronfman, Samuel, 156
Browder, Earl, 33-34
Brown, H. Rap, 89
bugging, 4, 63, 66-68, 132
Bureau of Criminal Alien Investigation, *see:*Bureau of Special Services, 24
Bureau of Special Service and Information (BOSSI), his-

tory of, 3-9; policy for, 10-13; 19, function, 20-21; 24-25, 27, responsibility of, 14-23, 26-28; history of, 24-25; personnel, 29-45; administration, 45-49; subversion and, 51-95; visitors' security, 96-120; relations with labor-management, 121-37; liaisons with other agencies, 138-51; recommended administrative controls of, 152-70

Burgess, Guy, 60

Butler, Norman 3X, 86

C

Carrington, Wayne, 165-66

Castro, Fidel, 25, 34, 69-71, 98, 101, 149

Caulfield, John, 71

"cell system," 58, 73

Central Intelligence Agency (CIA), 7, 29, 34, 40, 47, 49-51, 60, 62, 77, 90, 95, 120, 142, 144, 146, 151, 160-61

Central Office Bureaus and Squads (COBS), 150

Central Operations Center (BOSSI), 119

Certificate of Incorporation, 59

Chicago Police Department, 22

Chief Inspector (NYCPD), 31

Chief of Detectives (NYCPD), 19, 29, 32, 44, 150

Chief of Patrol (NYCPD), 32

Church, Frank, 161

Civil Liberties Union, 53

civil rights movement, 26-27, 51, 54, 74, 86

Code of Criminal Behavior, 146

Cold War, 4

Collier, Robert S., 76-78

Collins, Mae, 85

Columbia University, 91

Columbo, Joseph, 114

commanding officer (BOSSI), 6, 7, 26, 29-31, 36, 40-41, 58, 112, 147, 150-51

Committee to Reelect the President, 160

communism, 4, 16, 24-26, 71-73, 82,

Communist Party, 24, 33-34, 121, 142

community relations, 83, 155-57

"concentric ring" security, 110

Condon-Waldin Act, 125

Congress of Racial Equality, 75-76, 165

Counter Intelligence Corp., 114

covert operations, 6, 32, 62-69, 153

Criminal Procedure Law, 67

D

de Galindez, Jesus, 5, 91-93

de la Maza, Octavio, 92

de Gaulle, Charles, 99-100

demonstrations, 3, 4, 11, 16, 20, 46, 54-56, 107, 111, 136, 139, 145, 155, 165-66, 168

Department of Welfare (New York City), 125-27

De Pugh, Robert Bolivar, 72

"desk system," 107-09, 149

Detective Division (NYCPD), 19, 29, 42, 150

Diem, Ngo Dinh, 99

dignitaries, 16, 28, 46, 48, 96-120, 139
Diplomat Hotel, 166,
Dorticos Torrado, Osvaldo, 71, 108
dossiers, 9, 10, 58, 106, 113, 164
Duclos, Michele, 77
Dulles, Allen, 43, 45, 47, 56
Duncan, Abraham, 168

E

Ehrlichman, John, 71
Emergency Services Division (NYCPD), 111
employees rights (in strikes), 122, 129, 131-33
employers rights (in strikes), 122, 131
Epton, William, 81-82
Era of Trujillo, The, 91
evaluation (personnel), 43-45
Executive Action Committee, 160
executive officer (BOSSI), 32, 47
Executive Order #10450, 140
exiles, 4, 16, 37, 97, 101-02, 107-08, 112, 114

F

Fair Employment Practice Laws, 131-32
Fair Play for Cuba Committee, 149
Faisal, King (Iraq), 99
Faisal, King (Saudia Arabia), 99
Fard, W.D., 84
Federal Bureau of Investigation (FBI), 7, 22, 25, 27, 34, 50-51, 60, 77, 94-95, 101, 113, 117-18, 120, 123, 140-42, 144, 148, 151, 160-61, 164
FBI National Academy, 40
Federal Communications Commission, 68
Ferguson, Herman, 167
files (BOSSI), 9, 11, 48, 106, 113, 143, 150-52, 169
First National City Bank, 167
Ford, Gerald, 111, 116, 142
Fording, Addison H., 54
Foster, William Z., 122
Fox, Harry G., 158
Franco, Francisco, 91
Fraunce's Tavern, 7, 8
Freedom of Information Act, 94, 152
Freedom of Information Law, 169
Fromme, Lynnette Alice, 116

G

Gandhi, Mahatma, 99
Gangster Squad, *see*: Radical Squad, 24
Garfield, James, 98
Garilek, Sanford, 5, 6
Garvey movement, Marcus, 84
Gilligan, Thomas, 82
Guevara, Ernest "Che," 69-71

H

Harlem Defense Council, 82
Harlem riot (1964), 21-22, 82-83, 157
Harlem riot (1967), 35, 156-57
Harris, Arthur, 167
Hart, Abe, 83, 90
Hearst, Patricia, 11, 156

Helms, Richard, 47
Hitler, Adolph, 99-100, 134
Hoff, William, 165
Hoffa, James, 11
Hoffa v. United States, 79
homosexuality, 40, 92
Hoover Commission, 146
Hoover, J. Edgar, 22-23, 51, 115, 161
Howlette, Edward, 168
Hubbard, Timothy L., 166
Hussein, Abdullah Ibn, 99
Huston Plan, 23

I

identification, 9, 58, 60-61, 101, 108-09, 133
Industrial Squad, *see:* Radical Squad, 24
infiltration, 4, 32, 34-35, 46, 64, 74, 77, 79-81, 94, 156, 166
informants, 63
Inspectional Services Bureau, 152
Inspections Division, 5, 152
intelligence, 3, 4, 7, 12; policy on, 12-13; definition of, 18-19; 20-22, 27; operations for, 29, 56-60, 126-7, 134-37, 145-48, 156, 158-59; recommendations for future uses of, 160-170
Intelligence Division, 152
Internal Affairs Division, 152-53
International Association of Chiefs of Police, 87, 148, 152, 158
Intro bills (780, 781, 782), 161-63, 165-68
Irish Nationalists, 8

J

Jamaica Rifle and Pistol Club, 168
Jamaica Savings Bank, 168
Johnson, Lyndon, 113
Jones, Leroi, 168

K

Kassem, Abdal Karim, 99
Kefauver, Estes, 123
Kennedy, John F., 27, 85, 98, 101, 110, 113, 117, 119, 161
Kennedy, Robert, 123
Kent State University, 155, 163-64
Khrushchev, Nikita, 98, 111, 114
Knapp Commission, 68-69
Knapp, William, 5-7
King, Jr., Martin Luther, 94, 98, 160-61, 163-64
Krogh, Egil, 60
Ku Klux Klan, 94

L

labor disputes, 17-18, 29-30, 45, 48, 60-61, 121, 137-38, 164
language ability, 38, 108
Lewis v. United States, 79
liaisons, 28, 97, 118, 138-51
Life, 5, 86
Lincoln, Abraham, 98
Lincoln, C. Eric, 86
Lindsay, John V., 5, 6, 118
Lomax, Louis, 88-89, 156
Lumumba, Patrice, 99

M

McCarthy, Joseph, 93, 148

McClure, Brook, 164
McCone Report, 21, 27, 158-59
McCord, James, 71
McKinley, William, 98
McLean, Donald, 60
McManus, George P., 61
McQuillan, Peter, 78-79
Malcolm X Little, 5, 74, 81, 84-91, 94-95, 168
Manson, Charles, 116
Melville, Sam, 167
Minutemen, 4, 16, 25, 32, 53, 72-74, 77
monitoring, 134, 165, 170
Moore, Sara Jane, 116
Motormen's Benevolent Association, 132
Muhammad, Elijah, 16, 52, 84, 94-95
Muhammad, Wallace, 52, 84, 86, 87
Municipal Police Administration, 17, 133
Murphy, Gerry, 92
Murphy, Michael J., 112
Murphy, Patrick V., 6

N

Nassar, Abdul, 98
Nation of Islam, 52, 84-87
National Association for the Advancement of Colored People, 167
National Guard, 154-55, 164
Nationalist Party of Puerto Rico, 53
Neutrality Squad, *see*: Bureau of Special Services, 24, 78
New York City Charter, 14
New York City Council, 161, 163, 168
New York City Police Department (NYCPD), 4, mandate of, 14-15; 16, 18, 25, 29, 31, 36, 43, 47, 51, 64, 75, 87, 93, 96-97, 102, 114-16, 128-30, 136-37, 139-40, 145, 147-48, 151-52
New York State Penal Code, 52
New York State Police, 141
New York State Supreme Court, 67, 78, 162
New York *Times*, 10, 77
Nixon, Richard, 23, 67, 71, 111, 119
Novo, Guillermo, 70
Novo, Ignacio, 70

O

Olympio, Sylvanus, 99
Operations Center (NYCPD), 47, 137
Organization of Afro-American Unity (OAAU), 85
organized crime, 11, 28, 69, 114, 122-23, 139, 148, 163
Organized Crime Unit (NYCPD), 114
Osborn v. United States, 79
Oswald, Lee Harvey, 101, 117, 149
OTIS I.Q. test, 38
overt operations, 29, 34-35, 48, 56-61, 153
oversight committee, 151, 161, 170

P

Palestine Liberation Organization, 8
Palmer, Robin, 167
Penal Code (New York City

Charter), 146
Perez, Julio Carlos, 70
Personnel Records Unit, 42
Philadelphia Police Department, 158
Philby, Adrian Russell, 151
picketing, 46, 60-61, 122, 125, 127, 132-33, 135-36
Police Academy, 77, 141, 149
Police Administration, 148
Police Commissioner (NYCPD), 31
police corruption, 68-69, 153
police strike, 133-34
Poole, Elijah, *see*: Muhammad, Elijah
Pope Paul VI, 98
Porter, Charles O., 92
Powell, James, 82
President's Commission on Civil Disorders, 154
President's Commission on Law Enforcement and Administration of Justice, 138
President's National Crime Commission, 66, 68, 148
Princeton University Educational Testing Service, 40
proactive response model, 12, 127, 145
Progressive Labor Movement, 53, 81-83
Prohibition, 24
Public Law 357, 96
Public Relations Squad, *see*: Bureau of Special Services, 24, 78
Puerto Rican Independents, 8
Puerto Rican Nationalists, 4, 7, 16, 25, 37, 53, 100, 145

R

Radical Bureau, *see*: Bureau of Special Services, 24, 78
Radical Squad, *see*: Bureau of Special Services, 24
reactive response model, 12, 127
recruitment, 37-40, 149, 153
Remon, Jose, 99
Red Squad, The, *see*: Bureau of Special Services, 3, 147
Revolutionary Action Movement, 4, 32, 76-77, 155, 168
Revolutionary Council, 34
riots, 21, 27, 34-35, 82, 88-89, 153-59
Rockefeller Commission Report, 80
Rockefeller, Nelson, 118
Rockwell, Lincoln, 5, 53, 148
Rules and Procedures (R&P), 25-26, 128-30, 146

S

Sayyed, Khaleel S., 76
Secret Service, 27, 96, 101, 103-04, 106, 109-10, 114, 116-18, 138, 141
security, 16, 23, 27-28, 35, 48, 69, 71, 96-120, 138, 140, 142
sergeant's exam, 43
Shapiro, Irwin, 70
Shaw, George Bernard, 97
Skousen, W. Cleon, 30, 55, 61
Social Services Employees Union, 125-27
Somoza, Anastasio, 99
Sorge, Richard, 60
Spanish Civil War, 91
Statue of Liberty plot, 4, 32, 64, 76, 165
Stone, Donald C., 124
strikes, 17, 28, 122-37, 154
student movement, 54

Students for a Democratic Society, 25
subversion, 8, 21; definition of, 22; 23-28, 30, 45, 48, 51-95, 97, 140, 144, 146, 158, 164
Sukarno, 98
Symbionese Liberation Army, 8, 11

T

Tactical Patrol Unit (NYCPD), 41
targets (of investigation), 4, 5, 32, 56, 58-59, 63, 71, 98, 114, 162, 165
task forces, 28, 139
terrorism, 3, 7-9, 11, 17, 55, 58, 63, 74, 81, 117, 154-55, 159, 164, 168
Tito, Josif, 98
training (for BOSSI), 42, 44
Transport Workers Union, 132
Trujillo, Rafael, 25, 91-93, 99, 102-04
Truman, Harry S., 100
twenty-four hour log, 46-47

U

Ulasewicz, Anthony, 71
undercover agents, 46, 63-65, 79-88, 165, 167
U.F. 35 (Strike Report), 128
U.F. 57 process, 41, 153
union movement, 121-23
United Nations, 4, 15, 56, 69-72, 96-98, 102, 106-08, 112, 139
U.S. Congress, 11, 62, 96, 146, 160
U.S. Constitution, 53

U.S. Department of Defense, 114
U.S. Department of State, 102, 114, 116, 139-40
U.S. Department of the Treasury, 118
U.S. Immigration and Naturalization Service, 18-19, 28, 143
U.S. Internal Revenue Service, 50
U.S. Public Law 357, 96
U.S. Senate Select Committee on Intelligence, 47, 161, 163-64, 170
U.S. Supreme Court, 68
United States v. Russell, 79
Urban League, 167

V

Verwoerd, Hendrick Frensch, 99
Vietnam War, 3, 53, 163, 166-167

W

Wagner Act, 131
Wagner, Robert F., 75
Walsh, Timothy J., 134
Warren Commission, 17, 23, 99, 101, 115, 117-19, 148
Watergate, 7, 10, 13, 23, 50, 71, 77, 93, 118, 132, 142 144, 146, 160, 163, 170
Watts riot, 21-22, 27, 155-56, 158-59
weapons statutes, 52, 74
Weiner, Steve, 167
White, Ralph, 166
Wilkins, Roy, 76, 167-68
Williams, Robert F., 74
Wilson, O.W., 20, 22, 32, 148

wiretapping, 4-5, 40, 63, 66-68, 160, 162-63
Wise, David and Thomas B. Rose, 62
women, 37, 65
Wood, Raymond, 64, 75-76, 90, 165
"work in," 125
World War I, 27
World War II, 3, 24, 72, 96, 142, 163

Y

Yom Kippur War, 12
Young, Whitney, 76, 167-68

Z

Zelano, Frank, 132